ROB KRIER

Architectural Monographs No 30

ROB KRIER

ARCHITECTURE AND URBAN DESIGN

A.D. ACADEMY EDITIONS · E·S ERNST & SOHN

This book is dedicated to my parents
Maudy and Jempy Krier
They protected my dreams

Architectural Monographs No 30
Editorial Offices: 42 Leinster Gardens London W2 3AN

Editor: Richard Economakis; Editorial and Design Team: Andrea Bettella (Senior Designer); Jason Rigby,
Gina Williamson, Meret Gabra-Liddell (Design); Nicola Hodges, Iona Spens (Editorial)

Author's Note

I should like to express my gratitude to the Academy Group for their support and enthusiasm in publishing this monograph
on my work. I am especially grateful to Dr Andreas Papadakis for initiating the idea of a published 'oeuvre complete'. At
Academy Editions I should like to thank Richard Economakis for his editorial work; Andrea Bettella for his design and
technical advice; designers Jason Rigby, Gina Williamson and Meret Gabra-Liddell; and the editorial team Nicola Hodges
and Iona Spens. Special thanks go to Pamela Johnston for her work in translating my texts; thanks also go to Elena Ponte
for helping to translate the many captions. At my institute at the Technical University of Vienna, the support of my assistants
Johannes Kräftner, Valter Cernek and Claus Zwerger was invaluable as was the enthusiasm of the many talented people
who have worked with me for over 26 years; a very special mention to my junior partner and son-in-law Christoph Kohl;
last and not least, thanks to my daughter Nadine Krier who made the first lay-out sketch for the book and works passionately
as my house photographer having taken over from Johannes Kräftner, my senior assistant. Johannes is also one of the most
prominent architectural photographers in Austria having documented all my work from 1976 to 1990.

Cover: The new square in front of Notre Dame Cathedral, Amiens; *p2:* R Gruetzke, Portrait Sketch of Rob Krier

First published in Great Britain in 1993 by
ACADEMY EDITIONS
An imprint of the Academy Group Ltd

ACADEMY GROUP LTD
42 Leinster Gardens London W2 3AN
ERNST & SOHN
Hohenzollerndamm 170, 1000 Berlin 31
Members of VCH Publishing Group

ISBN 1 85490 204 0 (HB)
ISBN 1 85490 205 9 (PB)

Distributed to the trade in the United States of America by
ST MARTIN'S PRESS
175 Fifth Avenue, New York, NY 10010

Printed and bound in Singapore

CONTENTS

6

FOREWORD

To have credibility in the eyes of young people, a teacher must be able to tie theory to practice. Some individuals are able to communicate an encyclopedic knowledge with passion and conviction, but in our field that is not enough. The art of architectural composition is illustrated by the example of models: its theories must take into account the laws of construction and the logic of internal planning. As an applied art, building needs a foundation that remains valid beyond individual displays of architectural bravura. My own work is an attempt to uncover the different facets of this architectural 'truth'.

My main area of concern has been urban development. The great hopes and promises of the pioneers of the Modern Movement were not fulfilled – as we well know. Holding to their arrogant, naive belief that each generation had to invent anew the themes of the city and architecture, the Modernists practically made it a crime to refer back to the experience of the past. My projects were quickly categorised by critics as old fashioned, reactionary and eclectic. I was told that they were 'not in keeping with the spirit of the age'. During this century, the environment has been exploited on an unprecedented scale: we have seen more destruction, more power, than ever before. Our aggressive society and culture is reflected in the unbending form of the modern city – which I reject, sadly, and with bitterness. This abbreviated selection of works expresses my criticism of the much-praised 'spirit of the age'.

My brother Leo has played a decisive role in my artistic development over the past 30 years. Possessing quite different talents and temperaments, we have found ourselves inexplicably on the same track, and have argued about how to realise our shared conception of architecture. For a long time I found his unswerving, uncompromising attitude hard to understand, as I personally am not capable of such single-mindedness. Whereas Leo's whole, unblunted energy is directed towards architecture, I continue to waver – as indecisive as when I was 20 years of age – between architecture and sculpture. My vacillation means that my dreams of art always remain dreams. However, if you chew on a piece of tough meat for long enough, with enough determination, you are bound to digest something in the end. The sheer physical effort will bring its reward. And so I continue to work with these divided desires, hoping at the critical moment to draw a strength from the poetic stalemate that would make the struggle worthwhile.

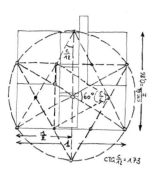  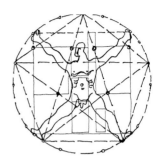

SIEMER HOUSE
STUTTGART, 1968

This was my first big commission after completing my studies. As usual, there was no money for either the architect or the house. But worse still, the client himself became creative – in a negative way – during the course of construction, and altered important details at whim. The result is that the house today looks like a ruin from the 1920s. The main building material is brick applied with a rough stucco render which is then painted. All the timber work, windows, doors and so on are painted in a deep bottle green. The paving at the ground level is large york stone. In plan the house is arranged symmetrically on either side of a skylit axis which contains the vertical circulation. The building is partly buried in the sloping site, giving the sense of a pristine object nestled into the surrounding nature. The idea of progression is emphasised both by the linear plan and vertically across the site through a series of stepped levels. These levels are echoed in the elevations which are sloped in the same direction as the terrain. The wedge-like appearance of the building permits large openings on the upper entrance facade and glimpses of the surroundings through the roof.

The building inevitably appears more imposing from the lower levels looking up as a result of the dramatic volumetric rises. It is both restrained and emphatic in its composition, setting itself up as a clear architectural statement with contextual sensitivity.

OPPOSITE: PLANS, ELEVATIONS AND ISOMETRIC PROJECTIONS OF THE PROJECT; *ABOVE:* COLOUR MODEL AND PROPORTIONAL DIAGRAMS; *BELOW:* VIEWS OF FACADES

Haus "Dickes"

10

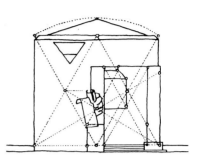

DICKES HOUSE
LUXEMBOURG, 1974

In keeping with the client's wishes, this house has few windows apart from the full-height openings oriented towards the terrace and the necessary light sources for the staircase and bathroom. The lady of the house had previously been pestered by a Peeping Tom and had no wish to repeat the experience here. The powerful architecture that arises from these requirements contrasts with the open plans of the interior. This 'living cell' could also be applied to row houses and larger building complexes. The walls are treated with a stucco render which is then painted. All the timber work, windows, doors and so on are painted in a deep bottle green. The paving at the ground level consists of large york stone slabs. A series of large oak beams are a feature of the ceiling at ground level and internally the roof of the hall is all in timber with a series of massive trusses left entirely visible. The building's simple volumetrics are its essence.

OPPOSITE: AXONOMETRIC COLLAGE SHOWING BUILDING IN THE ROUND; *FROM ABOVE L TO R:* PROPORTIONAL DIAGRAM; PROJECT MODEL; PROPORTIONAL DIAGRAM; VIEW OF THE BUILT PROJECT WITH SCULPTURE PHOTOMONTAGE; VIEW OF THE ENTRANCE FACADE

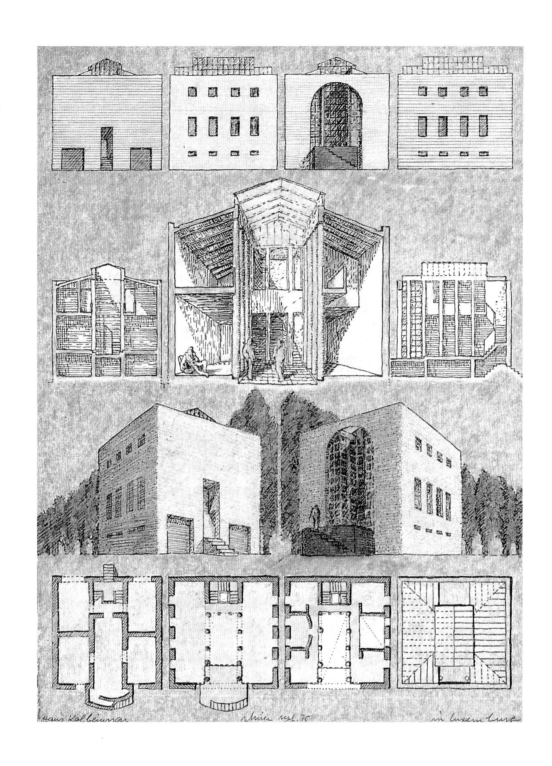

KOLBEINSSON HOUSE
LUXEMBOURG, 1975

In type, this house is reminiscent of the traditional basilica with nave and side aisles leading into each other. The hierarchic ground plan affords great flexibility without detriment to the central living area. The upper rooms also have an internal visual relation to the living room. The glass roof creates an atmosphere similar to that of a stretch of street or an inner court. Not unlike the Dickes House, this building is meant to be understood as an object with simple, solid facades and limited architectural 'events'. The large arched opening permits views outwards, yet allows the exterior to push, or penetrate into the building in the form of an open court. The house can be read both as a solid block and U-shaped plan, thus betraying, as it were, its nature as an exercise in 'controlled' typological complexity.

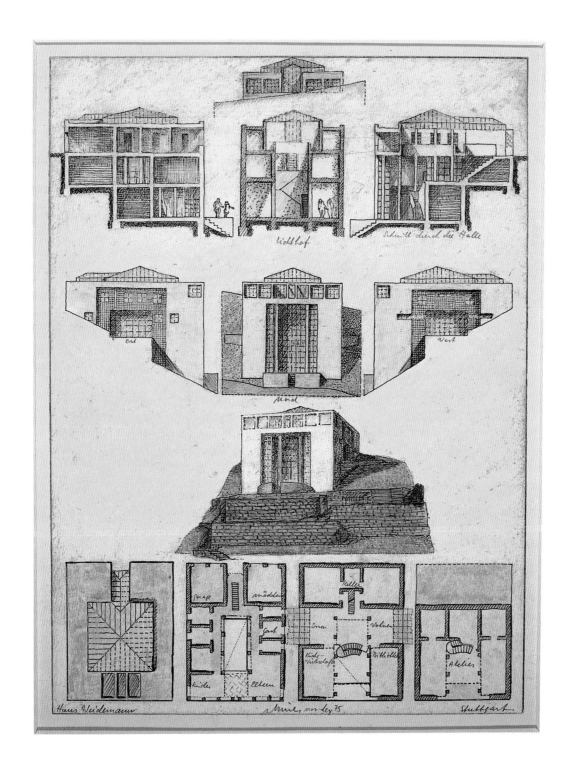

WEIDEMANN HOUSE
STUTTGART, 1975

This house was to be built with a graphics workshop on a very steep terraced northern slope. The design was rejected by the contractor because of it's 'monumentality'. In type, it is similar to the Kolbeinsson house. The storey with the living accommodation has a clear east-west orientation which continues on the terraces. The steps of the slope are also manifest in the three-storey space (inner court) above the studio. They are linked with various kinds of stairs. As with the Dickes and Kolbeinsson houses, the Weidemann House is chiefly an exercise in simple volumetric composition. The plan here, too, is symmetrically arranged around a long atrium or skylit court which contains the staircase in the upper levels. Openings are treated as simple cut-outs that do not interfere with the reading of the solid volumes out of which they are cut. The larger architectural moves are simplified, centralised patterns which emphasise the essential symmetry of each facade.

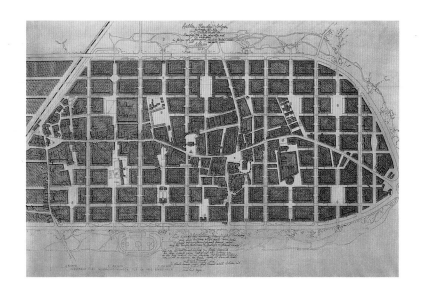

MASTERPLAN OF AALTER
BELGIUM 1966

Old Aalter is a typical linear village with a main street that widens in front of public buildings, and some cross-streets. It consists mainly of single-family row houses. The housing type I proposed matched the scale of the existing structures and was intended to blend into the old fabric. The masterplan as proposed envisages a grid-like expansion of the town on either side of the curving main street. Each new block would consist of residential units arranged around the perimeter, enclosing an open space. In order to ensure continuity and an efficient use of space, individual units were conceived as linear, two-storey volumes which straddle the smaller streets. The effect would not be unlike the medieval passages and vaulted streets that permeate vernacular settlements. At regular intervals large open squares and greens would act as neighbourhood centres, contrasting with the density of the urban blocks. Within each block a system of garden walls ensures that residents have a high degree of privacy, while benefitting from the large openings and well-lit courts.

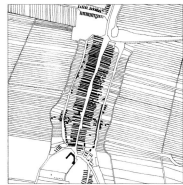

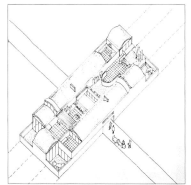

FROM ABOVE L TO R: MASTERPLAN OF AALTER; VIEW OF MODEL; TYPICAL LINEAR VILLAGE IN BURGERLAND; MODEL OF LIGHTWEIGHT ADAPTABLE FLOOR
CONSTRUCTION; ISOMETRIC UNITS STRADDLING STREETS

LEINFELDEN
STUTTGART 1971

This condensed complex containing around 1,000 flats and extensive office, administrative and commercial facilities was intended to provide the town of Leinfelden with a new centre – a definite focus for the community. The site of the railway and underground stations was chosen because no inspiration for a spatially considered urban development could be found in the existing heterogeneous residential centre with its detached houses. The extremely narrow, elongated nature of the site called for a linear development.

The functional and spatial focal points of the scheme are the town hall, with its cultural and social facilities, the railway and underground stations, a shopping centre, and a weekly market-place. These are set into a three-part spatial sequence: the town hall square; the shopping gallery with access to the stations through two small courtyards; and the square for the weekly market. The different elements are linked by a single axis, which provides the foundation for any future development of the town centre.

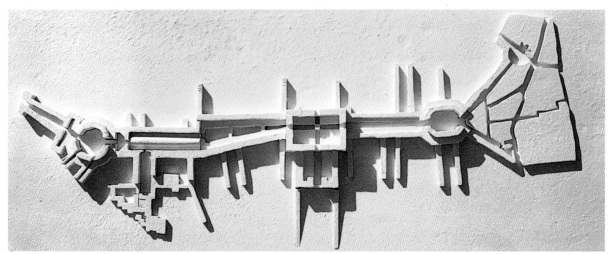

FROM ABOVE: AERIAL PERSPECTIVE WITH PLANS AND VIEWS OF THE PROJECT; MODEL OF THE SCHEME; COURTYARD VIEWS

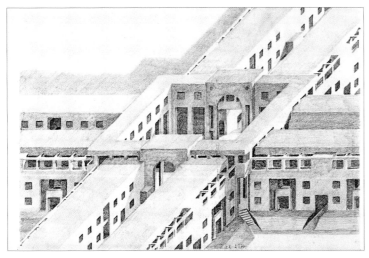

ROYAL MINT SQUARE
LONDON, 1974

This project falls within the London Docklands redevelopment area. The basic architectural fabric is exceptionally rich and adaptable to other urban functions; but unfortunately one of the most fascinating features of the area is being lost, as some of the old docks are filled in.

My sketches showing an ideal project were based on the assumption that existing buildings would be retained and converted to new uses wherever practicable. The old fabric is integrated into the new development. The structure of the blocks themselves could be filled out at a later date. The project plan is cruciform with a large square at the centre from

which radiate four 'streets' with residential blocks arranged to form urban facades. These facades are treated as continuous surfaces with localised openings and architectural events. Entrances are treated as 'inserted' elements in larger voids. Spacious balconies and terraces look out over landscaped gardens at the back of the street houses, not unlike the traditional English terraces. The central square is meant to act as a focal point for the entire project, on which residents can converge socially. Continuous arcades line the street fronts and give the complex a traditional urban character, leading, at the same time, into the open square.

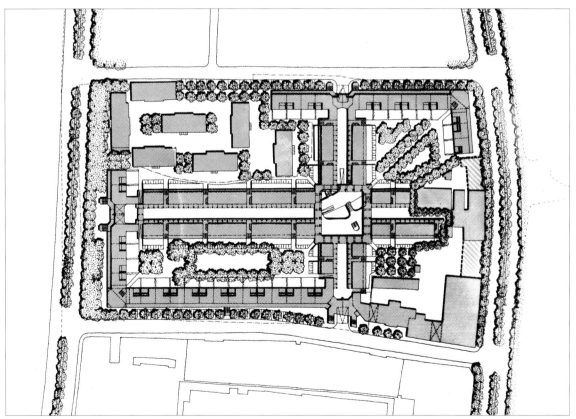

OPPOSITE ABOVE: STREET ELEVATION; *OPPOSITE BELOW:* SKETCHES FOR AN ARCHITECTURAL INTERPRETATION OF THE URBAN SPACES INSIDE THE BLOCK; *ABOVE:* VIEW OF THE CENTRAL COURT WITH BATTERSEA POWER STATION IN THE DISTANCE; *BELOW:* SITE PLAN

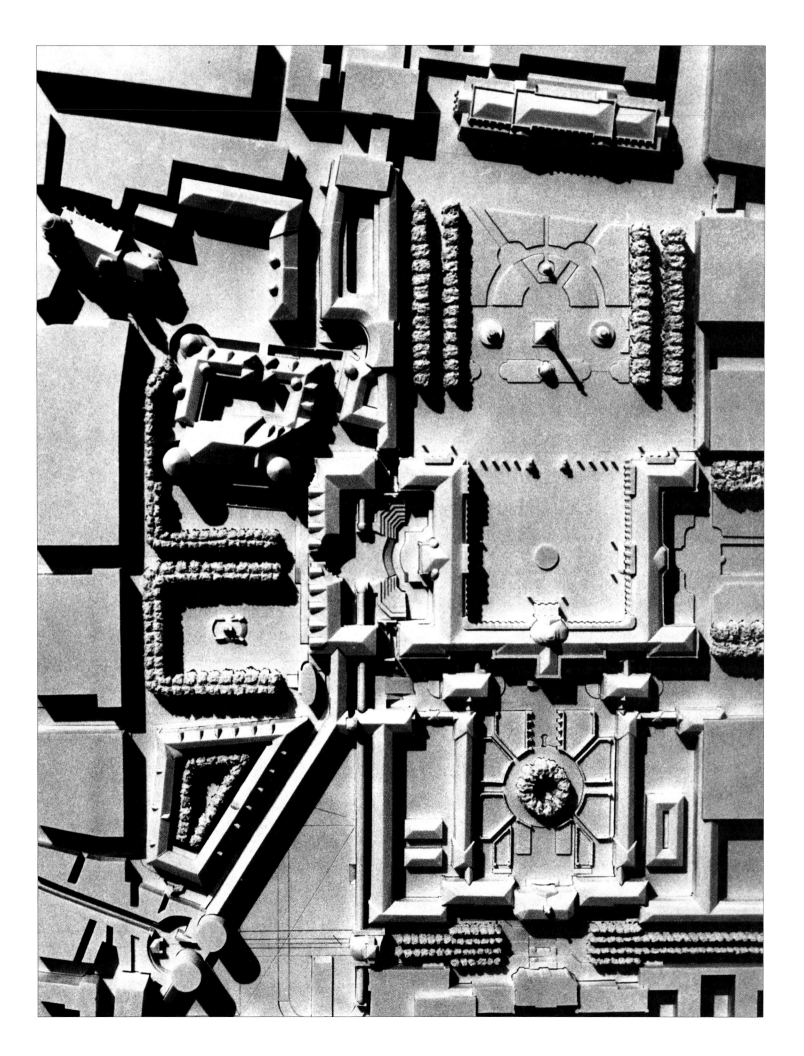

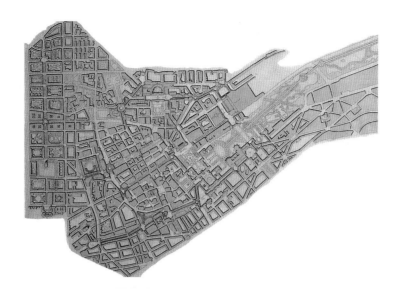

RECONSTRUCTION OF THE INNER CITY
STUTTGART, 1973

The inner city of Stuttgart has been characterised traditionally by an interplay between free-standing monuments, churches and palaces, and a continuous dense urban fabric. The concept behind the proposed reconstruction of this part of town is to maintain the traditional dialogue while creating new squares and streets. Buildings are used primarily as defining elements for the urban spaces which are alternatively landscaped or left as open fora. All the open spaces are connected to each other through a complex system of streets and covered passages which are designed in such a way as to lead the pedestrian from one to the other in a sequence of 'discoveries'. Thus, the triangular Charlottenplatz is bordered by a semi-circular 'forecourt' with flanking towers. Arcades emphasise the continuity of the street facades and further entice the visitor to explore the urban connections. An extended subway system connects the spaces at a lower level and facilitates commuting. As much as possible the original pre-war form of streets and squares has been preserved, as with the horse-shoe shaped Österreichischer platz. The complexity of old Stuttgart's plan serves as a model throughout the design process.

OPPOSITE: MODEL OF THE SITE AROUND THE CASTLE; *ABOVE:* AERIAL VIEW OF THE MODEL; *BELOW:* SITE PLAN

FROM ABOVE L TO R: MODEL OF THE NEW ÖSTERREICHISCHER PLATZ; VIEW OF THE HORSE-SHOE SHAPED ÖSTERREICHISCHER PLATZ; PLAN OF THE NEW ÖSTERREICHISCHER PLATZ; AERIAL VIEW OF THE ÖSTERREICHISCHER PLATZ

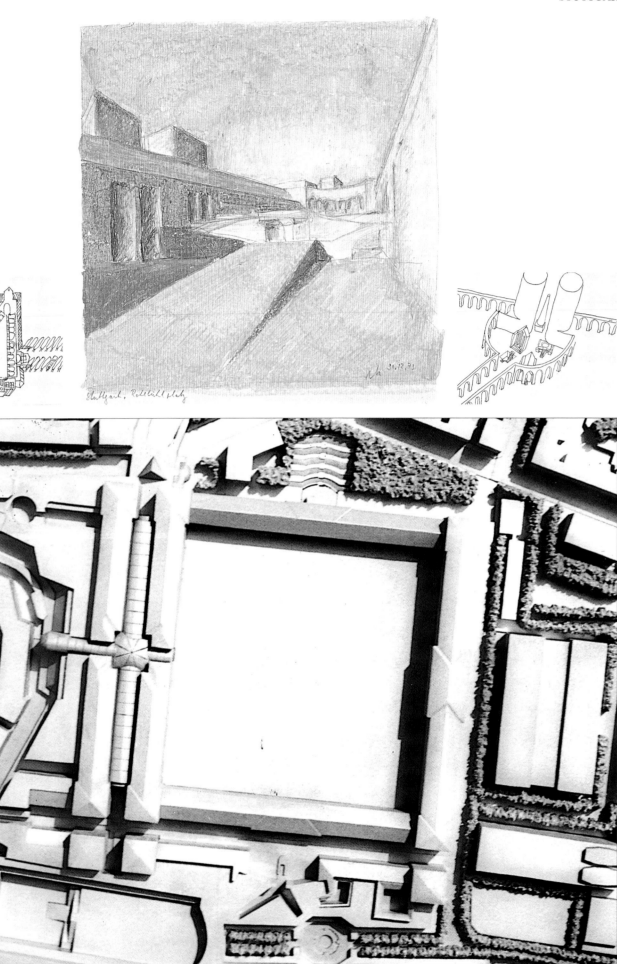

FROM ABOVE L TO R: SKETCH OF THE AMPHITHEATRICAL FORECOURT LEADING INTO CHARLOTTENPLATZ; SKETCH OF THE LINEAR SQUARE WITH THE ENTRANCE TO THE SUBWAY SYSTEM ON THE ROTEBÜHLPLATZ; SKETCH OF THE TRIANGULAR CHARLOTTENPLATZ; MODEL VIEW OF ROTEBÜHLPLATZ

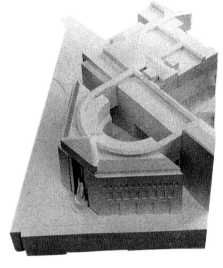
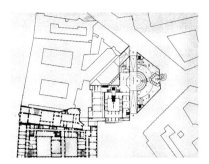

PROPOSAL FOR THE BALLHAUS PLATZ
VIENNA, 1976

The basic urban planning concept was to create a new street connecting the Hofburg (the residence of the Austrian President) with Minoritenplatz. By extending into the inner area of the building, the street also forms a communicating element between the general public and the government buildings.

The building form takes into consideration the historical typology, with particular regard for the existing scale and the significance of the site. In this way the new building offers an architectural solution which will maintain an enduring position in the urban composition. The entrance to the government building has been located at its natural focal-point at the street *intersection. It is announced by both the large sculpture and column which embodies the transformation of the vertical surfaces into free-standing support. The solidity and continuity of the surrounding urban fabric has been maintained in the elevation, employing simple openings and allowing the entrance to dominate as the primary focal point. A complex system of skylights crowns the building and suggests a more open interior than the elevations might imply. On the inside, in fact, one moves through the columned entrance lobby to discover the main auditorium, semi-circular in shape, which is connected to a large rectangular hall to the south.*

OPPOSITE: FACADE STUDIES OF BALLHAUSPLATZ AND DIALOGUE BETWEEN OLD AND NEW; *FROM ABOVE L TO R:* GROUND AND UPPER FLOORS OF THE PROJECT; MODEL VIEW OF PROJECT; AXONOMETRIC SKETCHES OF THE PROJECT

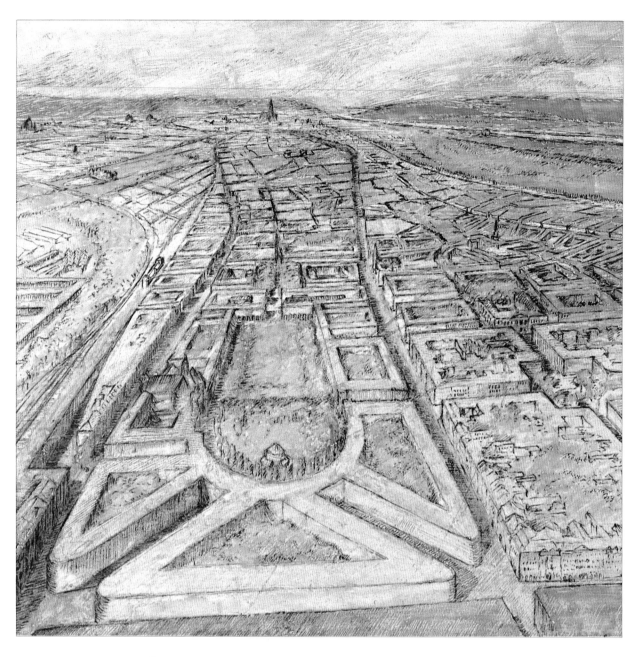

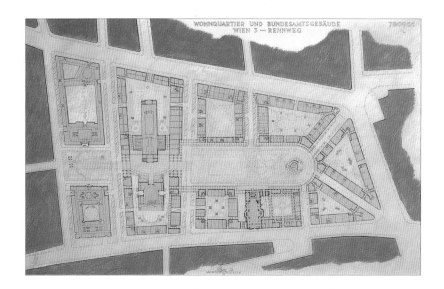

HOUSING ON THE RENNWEG
VIENNA, 1977

The task here was to restructure and extend a site that had previously contained barracks. The existing pattern of urban blocks in the area around the competition site was adopted as the correct strategy for subdividing the new quarter. The historical plan was taken into consideration and features of the existing fabric were incorporated so as not to eliminate at a stroke an urban development that had taken hundreds of years to form. These existing features contribute to the richness and individual character of the area.

Another assumption was that the existing old buildings would be incorporated into the new plan wherever feasible. The large cruciform plans of the barracks were subdivided with new buildings, creating new streets leading to a central green space. This square ends at the west with a crescent, five storeys high, upon which converge tree-lined streets. The continuity of the facades around the green provides a high degree of enclosure, broken only by the arched street entrances. The density of the urban blocks is thus ensured, while at the same time smaller inner courts, also landscaped, act as more private focal points for the individual housing units.

As the small study plans show, the primary concept guiding the design process was the preservation of the traditional urban fabric of Vienna and the incorporation at the heart of the development of a sizeable figural open space.

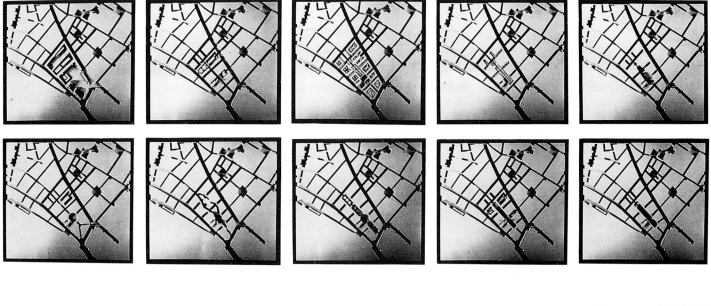

OPPOSITE, FROM ABOVE L TO R: AERIAL VIEW OF THE PROJECT; VIEW OF THE CRESCENT AT THE END OF THE GREEN; STREET VIEW;
ABOVE: SITE PLAN; *BELOW:* URBAN DEVELOPMENT SKETCHES FOR THE PROJECT

NEW COMMUNITY CENTRE
BRUNN AM GEBIRGE, VIENNA, 1977

This complex is meant to close the courtyard behind the town hall and create a spatially intact figure. The square main hall with surrounding corridors, the stage area, oval stairwell and the old hall form a sequence of spaces which develops from the foyer on the ground floor. The individual parts are geometrically differentiated and linked to the main room and surrounding area. The individual side walls emphasise the orientation and filter the light sources. The octagonal support of the oval glass-roofed staircase with its mushroom capital carries the landing on the upper store. The link between the staircase and the old hall is emphasised; the hall having been enriched with a gallery. A simple timber roof caps the main space which is conceived as a geometrically pure volume. Large arched openings on three sides strengthen the symmetrical plan.

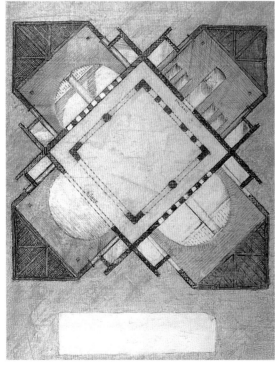

FROM ABOVE L TO R: AXONOMETRIC OF THE PROJECT; PLAN; OVAL STAIRCASE

URBAN PROPOSAL FOR ALTONA NORD
HAMBURG, 1978-81

This work was based on the following premises:
1. The proposal should complete the historical plan.
2. Urban space should be clearly defined in the geometric pattern of the streets and squares – the only zones of public interaction in modern urbanism.
3. The massing of the blocks should ensure the greatest possible transparency within the urban structure.

The basic principle behind this redevelopment was to subdivide the gigantic old blocks into smaller units in order to create a transparency within the urban structure. This transparency benefits everyone who lives in the city, not only the pedestrian but the motorist too. Indeed, it is the only means of halting the decay of the inner area of the blocks, which have lost their direct relationship to the public cityscape.

FROM ABOVE L TO R: SITE PLAN SHOWING THE URBAN SPACES; THE NEW BORDERS FOR THE GREEN NEXT TO THE OPERA HOUSE WITH THE PLAN SHOWING THE FOUR TOWERS HOUSING DOCTOR SURGERIES; RESIDENTIAL AND OFFICE BLOCK ON THE FORMER PFERDEMARKT WITH CIRCULAR COURT

AERIAL VIEW OF THE SITE

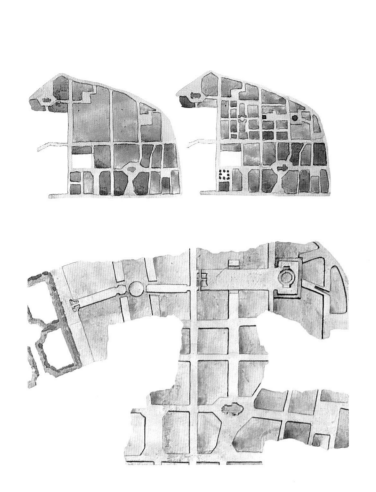

FROM ABOVE L TO R: DEVELOPMENT SKETCHES FOR THE URBAN PLAN; THE 'SCHILLER OPERA' YOUTH CENTRE;
THE ROUND SQUARE AT THE INTERSECTION OF THE OLD PEOPLE'S HOMES; VIEW OF BOLZPLATZ

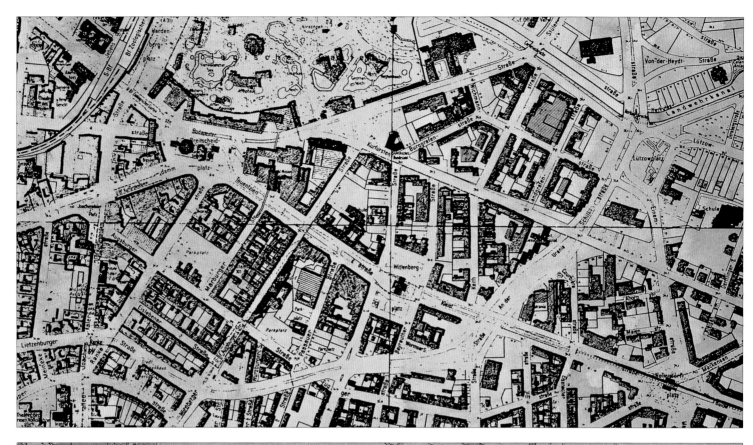

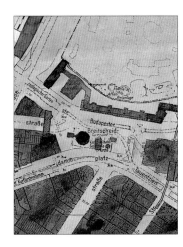
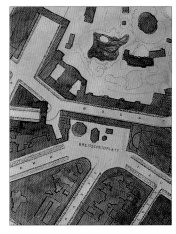

PROPOSAL FOR WEST BERLIN CITY CENTRE
1976-77

The Kurfürstendamm /Tanzentierstraße area was developed with Leon Krier. The programme invited a variety of approaches to restructuring this area. We decided to focus on two fundamental issues:

1. A critique of the structure of the centre of West Berlin (Leon's contribution).

2. A critique of the urban space and architectural quality of the area.

The area around the Breitscheidplatz was not conceived to be the centre of the city, but was developed as a suburb in the 19th century. Its large block patterns lack the essential features for an urban centre – notably a transparency and permeability for pedestrians and traffic. We wanted this project to illustrate the possibility of creating a more human spatial quality within this environment.

OPPOSITE, FROM ABOVE: EXISTING SITE PLAN; PROPOSED SITE PLAN; FROM ABOVE: EXISTING AND PROPOSED PLAN FOR BREITSCHEIDPLATZ; VIEW OF THE EXISTING SITE WITH BUSY INTERSECTION; MODEL OF BREITSCHEIDPLATZ

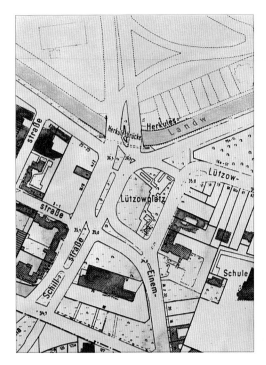
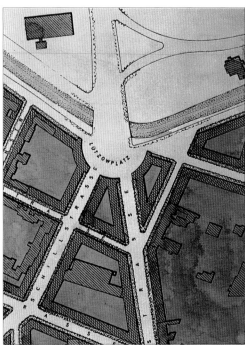

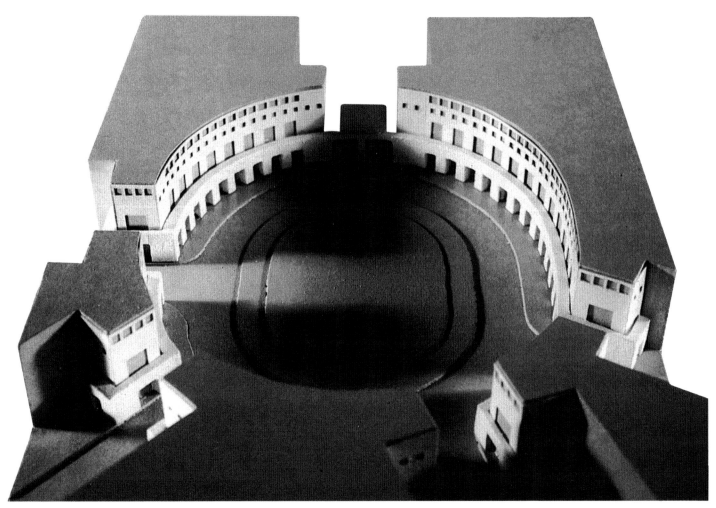

FROM ABOVE: EXISTING AND PROPOSED PLAN OF LÜTZOWPLATZ; MODEL OF LÜTZOWPLATZ

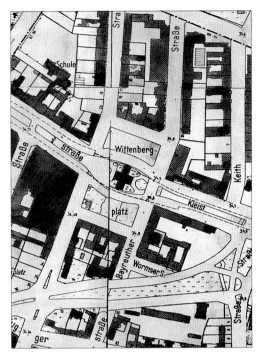
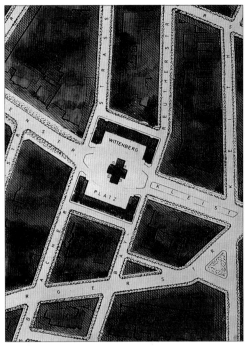

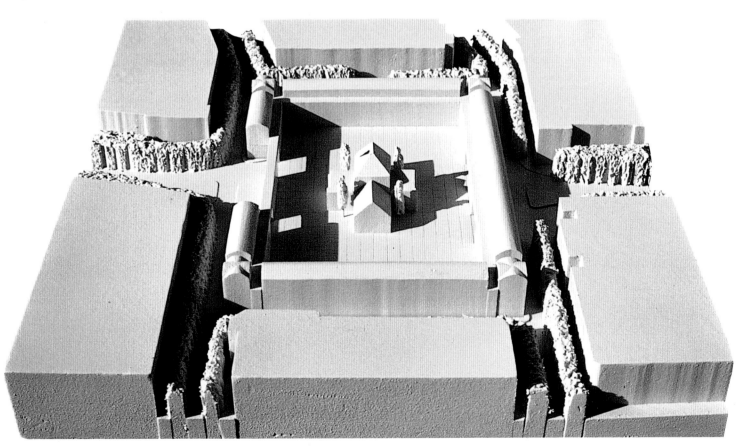

FROM ABOVE: EXISTING AND PROPOSED PLAN OF WITTENBERGPLATZ; MODEL OF WITTENBERGPLATZ

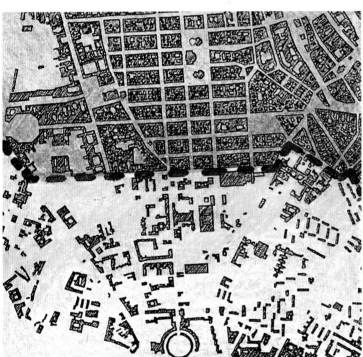
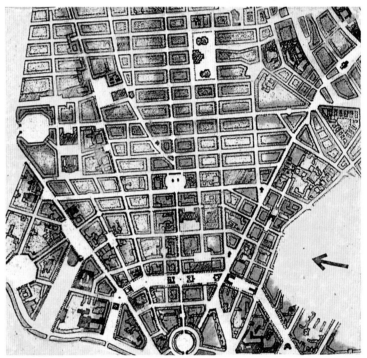

URBAN DEVELOPMENT OF SOUTH FRIEDRICHSTADT
BERLIN, 1977

The ideal plan for South Friedrichstadt in Berlin was based on the assumption that Berlin would not be divided forever between East and West and that the area between Mehringplatz and Unter den Linden should be treated as a single entity. I have re-adopted the 19th-century city plan, which was largely destroyed during the war and the subsequent rebuilding. An important element of this ideal plan is the landscaped 'ring of culture' which starts some way out from Mehringplatz, extend-

ing in a semicircle from the Museum of the City of Berlin. This 90 metres-wide ring is intended to contain the most important cultural buildings and to provide some much-needed green space. Care has also been taken to minimise disturbance of the existing fabric. The new post-war buildings fit in as best they can; later phases of the plan could improve their integration. It is important to limit building heights to a maximum of six storeys and to avoid any further high-rises.

OPPOSITE: SKETCH OF LEIPZIGERPLATZ WITH THE MONUMENT TO FREDERICK THE GREAT DESIGNED BY FR GILLY;
FROM ABOVE L TO R: SITE PLAN AT THE BEGINNING OF THE 19TH CENTURY; SITE PLAN IN 1975; SITE PLAN IN 1939; THE NEW PROPOSAL

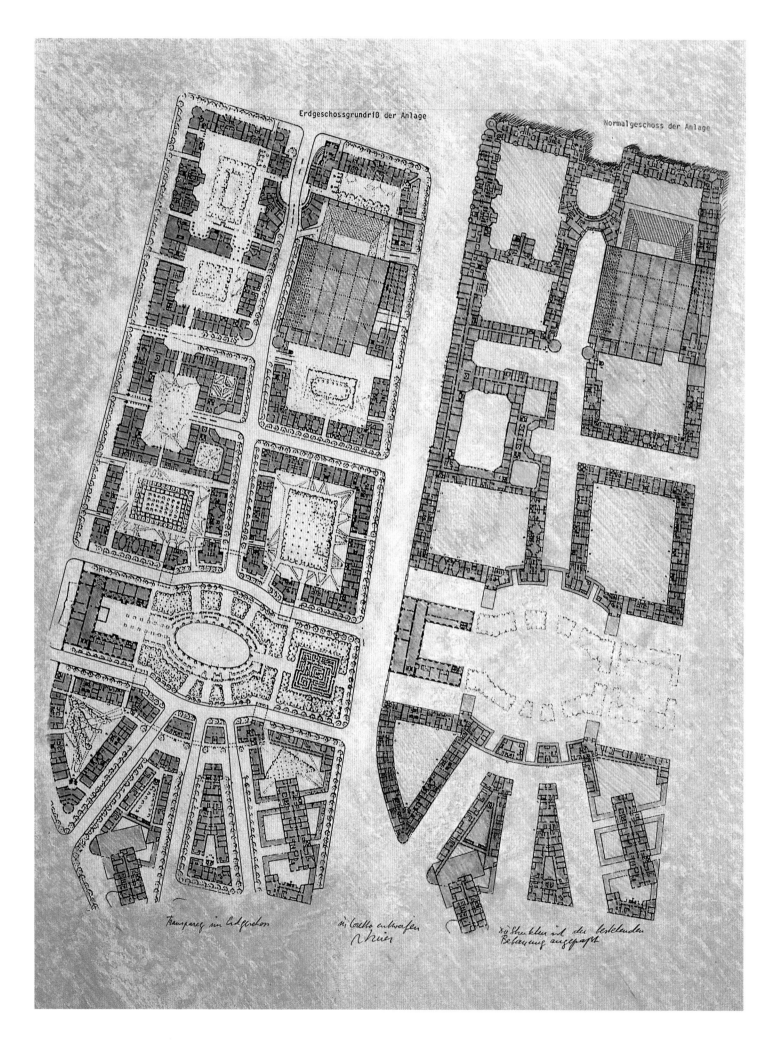

Erdgeschossgrundriß der Anlage

Normalgeschoss der Anlage

OPPOSITE: PLANS FOR THE BERLIN MUSEUM QUARTER, SOUTH FRIEDRICHSTADT; *FROM ABOVE:* SITE PLAN;
SKETCH OF THE SEMI-CIRCULAR COURT AT THE END OF THE CENTRAL AXIS

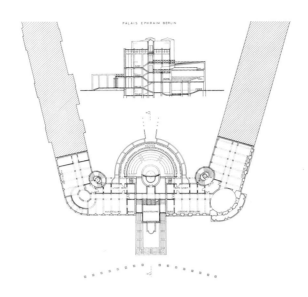

RECONSTRUCTION OF EPHRAIM PALACE
BERLIN, 1979

The right wing of the Palace stood in what is now the eastern part of the city, but was demolished before the war. After the war the numbered stones were rediscovered in West Berlin, and the Senate has now decided to rebuild the palace for the Jewish community and provide cultural facilities there. The work presents a special challenge in the handling of valuable historical material and the best approach would appear to be a plain solid structure with the same proportions as the old building. The junction of the old and new sections should be bridged with a glazed foyer and stairs. From the central part of the foyer zone a semi-circular lecture room projects into the courtyard area. Ramps are attached which link the

lecture hall with the garden. The main compositional element of the old palace was the oval salon with an oval staircase. I have attempted to create a 'twin' to its Baroque predecessor through a similar sequence on the new corner. The amphitheatrical lecture room opens at the lower level onto the landscaped gardens through spacious arched doors. The curved street corners with their elaborate porticoes are echoed on the rear facade in the shapes of the oval staircase towers; their skylit domes reflecting the larger glass domes over the salons. On the street facades the general arrangement and disposition of the old Palace's openings is maintained, albeit in a more simplified manner.

 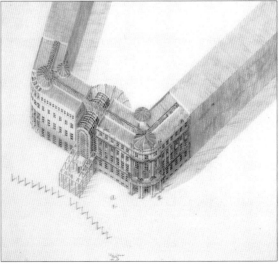

OPPOSITE: AXONOMETRIC PROJECTION OF STREET INTERSECTIONS, BERLIN MUSEUM QUARTER; *FROM ABOVE L TO R:* PLAN AND SECTION OF THE BUILDING; THE OLD PALACE AS IT APPEARED BEFORE THE WAR; AXONOMETRIC VIEWS OF THE PROPOSAL

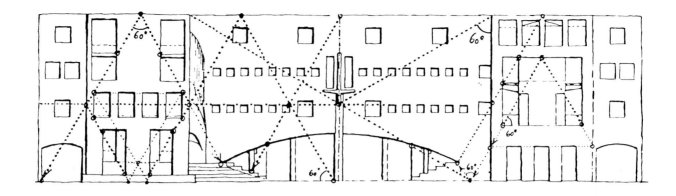

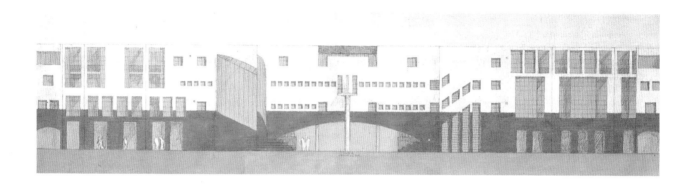

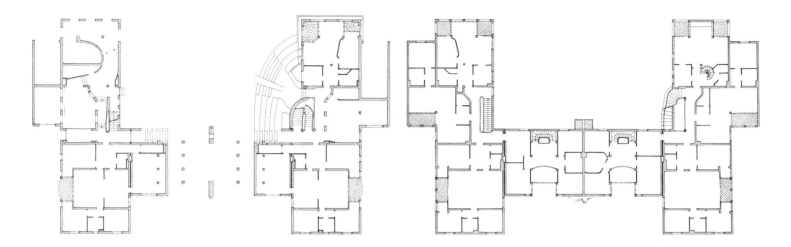

APARTMENT BUILDING IN RITTERSTRASSE
BERLIN, 1977-80

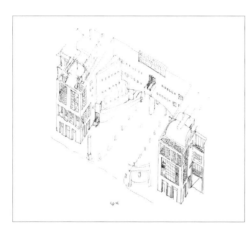

The building marks the centre of the northern edge of the block on Ritterstrasse. The projection of the facade, recessed forecourt and gateway signal the entrance to the interior of the block. There are plans to run a residential street from this point to the Berlin Museum, so the wings facing the courtyard are designed to allow for extension at a later date.

I have proposed that the edge of the block be subdivided into manageable plots for a number of reasons, most importantly:

1. To put a halt to fast-track production of housing by a single architect and so give work to other architects.
2. To re-establish small groups of housing which will again allow people to get to know their neighbours.
3. To create a small-scale architecture that is easy to recognise and orient oneself by.
4. To recognise that housing can only rise above the other functions of the city if it once again takes on the variety that in the past characterised, enlivened and enriched the streetscape.

OPPOSITE, FROM ABOVE: PROPORTIONAL SYSTEMS DETERMINING THE FACADE COMPOSITION; ELEVATIONS; VIEW FROM RITTERSTRASSE; *FROM ABOVE L TO R:* GROUND FLOOR PLAN; FIRST FLOOR PLAN; SKETCH OF THE PROJECT; VIEW FROM THE COURTYARD; VIEW FROM RITTERSTRASSE

OPPOSITE: THE FACADE COVERED IN IVY; *FROM ABOVE L TO R:* PLANS AND INTERIOR VIEW OF SIX-ROOM APARTMENT;
APARTMENT BASED ON A TURKISH GROUND PLAN; VIEW OF THE ENTRANCE FACADE

44

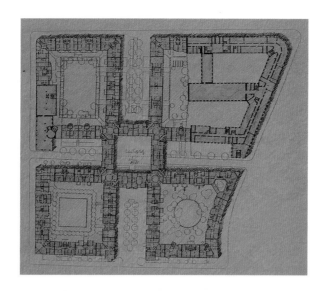

SCHINKELPLATZ
BERLIN, 1977-87

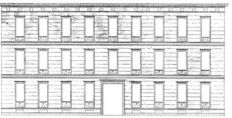

After examining a number of alternatives, I decided to give the square a regular form, enclosed on all sides. This provided a shield against the still derelict surrounding area and at the same time established an important spatial link between Mehringplatz and Oranienstrasse. The 30 metre² public square can be entered from the centre of all four sides. Additional passages from the corners lead to the landscaped courtyards of the housing. The courtyards are on a level 1.5 metre above the streets and squares, in order to minimise the length of the ramp needed to enter the underground parking. All the rooms are grouped around a central living space which is accessible from two sides, allowing the organisation of the flats to be adapted to any orientation: to the street, the square or the courtyard. The living room and loggia or winter garden are each situated in response to the orientation of the building – all that remains is for the children to be put in the sunniest spot. The central living rooms are varied in shape to give them distictive characters.

OPPOSITE: FACADE IN IMITATION OF SCHINKEL'S FEILNER BUILDING; *FROM ABOVE:* PLAN OF THE PROJECT; ELEVATION OF SCHINKEL'S FEILNER BUILDING; VIEW OF THE CENTRAL SQUARE, SCHINKELPLATZ

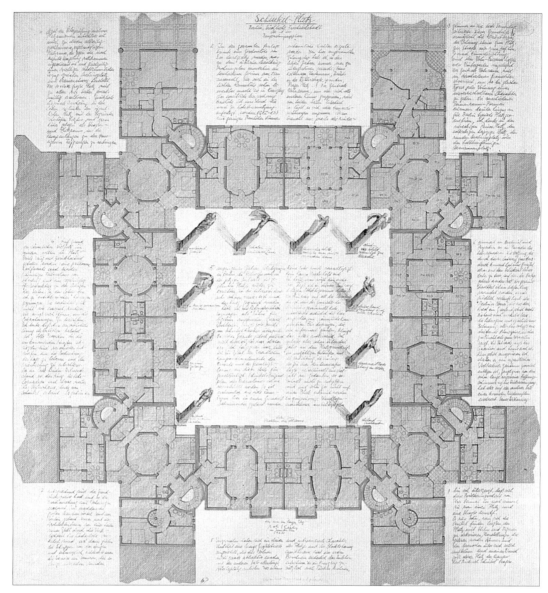

OPPOSITE: AXONOMETRIC SHOWING THE FACADE COMPOSITIONS WITH SKETCHES OF THE RESIDENTIAL ACCOMMODATION AROUND SCHINKELPLATZ; *FROM ABOVE L TO R:* DETAIL PLAN OF SCHINKELPLATZ; INTERIOR SKETCH OF RESIDENTIAL UNIT; OCTAGONAL LIVING ROOM

FROM ABOVE L TO R: WEST PORTICO; EAST PORTICO; ENTRANCE FROM RITTERSTRASSE; SOUTH PORTICO; NORTH PORTICO

FROM ABOVE L TO R: HOUSE 12 BY BRANDT, HEISS, LIEPE AND STEIGELMAN; HOUSE 11 BY BANGERT, JANSEN, SCHOLZ AND SCHULTES; HOUSES 20, 21, 19 BY BRANDT, HEISS, LIEPE AND STEIGELMAN; GANZ AND ROLFES; MÜLLER AND RHODE (RESPECTIVELY)

50

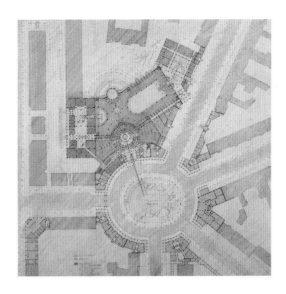

PRAGERPLATZ
BERLIN, 1978

The square still bears the marks of the war. I would suggest restoring the original ground plan as far as possible. The projections where the streets meet the square are to increase the architectural frontage. Moreover, the best apartments can be placed at these corners. In the interior of the block a large swimming pool is to be built, together with an adult education centre, a day nursery, library, restaurant etc. Here, too, the buildings are not to be designed by one architect but as in all my urban projects worked out in collaboration with several colleagues. As can be seen in the sketches of the interior, spaces are treated figurally as much as possible for the sake of architectural clarity. Glass skylighting in the form of domes, vaults and gables occurs over all the primary spaces, thus ensuring a high degree of natural lighting. Public spaces generally make a transition from solid wall to void through semi-solid colonnades and galleries. Spaces are thus enclosed by soft surfaces which set up an architectural dialogue. As with the Royal Mint, Schinkelplatz and the housing on the Rennweg projects, street facades are treated as continuous surfaces intended to maintain the historic urban fabric

OPPOSITE: SKETCHES FOR THE INTERIORS OF PRAGERPLATZ; *ABOVE:* SITE PLAN; *BELOW:* BIRD'S EYE AXONOMETRIC VIEW

Haus am Prager Platz
Berlin-Wilmersdorf

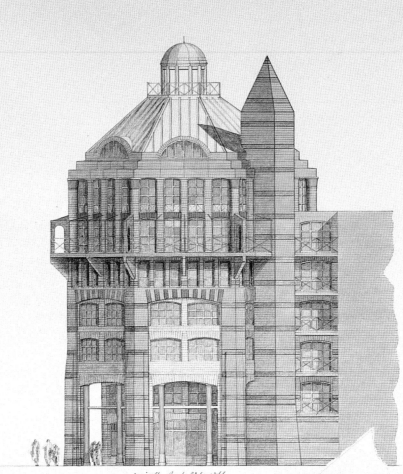

perspektive Nord-Südansicht

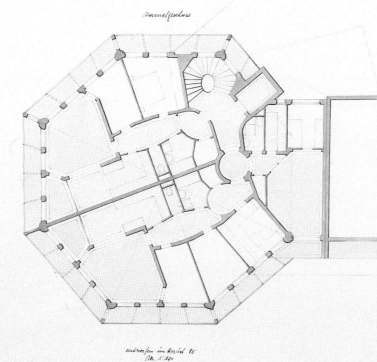

Normalgeschoss

entworfen im Herbst 85
M. 1:100
R. Krier

OPPOSITE: ELEVATION AND PLAN OF OCTAGONAL HOUSE, PRELIMINARY DESIGN; *ABOVE:* STUDIES OF HOUSE TYPES AT PRAGERPLATZ

HOUSE I
SPANDAU, BERLIN, 1978-81

These two buildings are part of a block on the edge of the medieval heart of Spandau, on the site of the fortifications which separated the city from the Havel river. The living spaces are oriented towards courtyard and street in order to take advantage of the natural light. The courtyard side overlooks the medieval roofscape of Spandau. The project, which provides social housing, was included in the plans of the 1984 Berlin International Building Exhibition (IBA). The Dutch architect Herman Hertzberger was invited to design the infill between the two buildings; other housing in the block is the work of the Berlin architects Jahn, Pfeiffer and Suhr. The buildings are of the same height, but each has its own character. I attempted to keep the massing simple while concentrating on the development and proportions of the individual elements.

FROM ABOVE L TO R: FLOOR PLAN; PLAN DIAGRAM; STREET FACADE; REAR FACADE

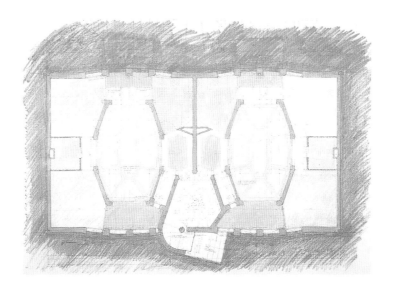

HOUSE II
SPANDAU, BERLIN, 1978-81

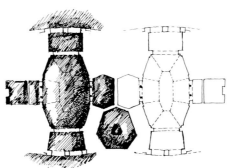

This design is built on the notion of a clear internal geometry. The organisation of the plan develops outwards from the living room, which takes the form of a compressed octagon. The hallway next to the living room is hexagonal, the staircase heptagonal. But the plan was not dictated by a fetish with geometry. The form of the adjoining rooms developed out of the form of the living room, the place where the family gathers, the 'heart of the house' (Leon Battista Alberti) which is wide in the middle, but narrower at either end to accommodate windows. This notional axis also gives the room a clear orientation towards the daylight ends. The terrace on the south side of the building provides a winter garden, and a good climatic buffer.

FROM ABOVE L TO R: FLOOR PLAN; PLAN DIAGRAM; STREET FACADE; REAR FACADE

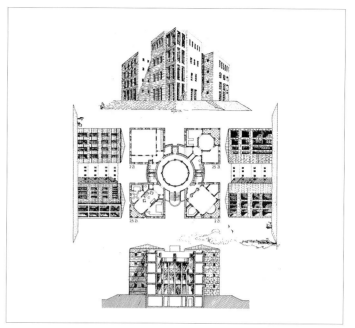

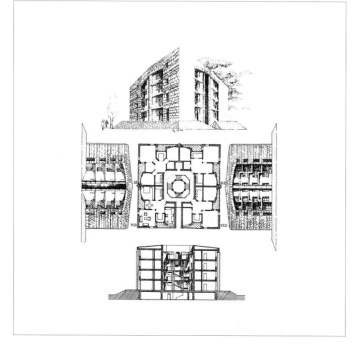
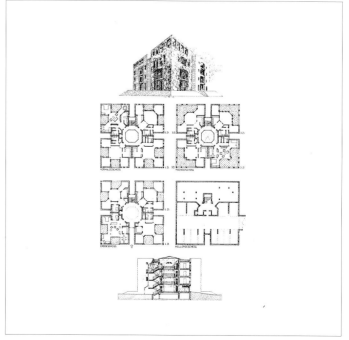

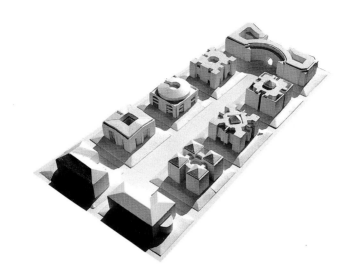

HOUSING ON THE TIERGARTEN
RAUCHSTRASSE, BERLIN, 1980

An urban-scale block would have been quite inappropriate for this site on the edge of a wonderful green space in the historically sub-urban Tiergarten. I therefore chose to put the new housing in individual buildings of a similar size to the old villas in the neighbourhood – the matching of scale is most evident in the semi-detached houses on the part of the old Stülerstrasse that is now known as Thomas-Dehler-Strasse. The hous-

ing is arranged around a central green, which is closed-off by a gateway from the busy Stülerstrasse. On the opposite side, on Drakestrasse, a similar spatial closure is formed by a pair of matched buildings, one of them the former Norwegian embassy. The intention is to relate each flat to the adjacent green space, whether public or private. An embankment one metre high and four metres wide wraps around the buildings.

OPPOSITE ABOVE AND BELOW: APARTMENT TYPES; *OPPOSITE CENTRE:* VIEW OF THE CRESCENT ON A BUSY DAY; VIEW LOOKING AWAY FROM THE CRESCENT; *FROM ABOVE:* VIEW OF THE MODEL; SCULPTURE AT THE ENTRANCE; VIEW OF THE CRESCENT FROM THE GREEN

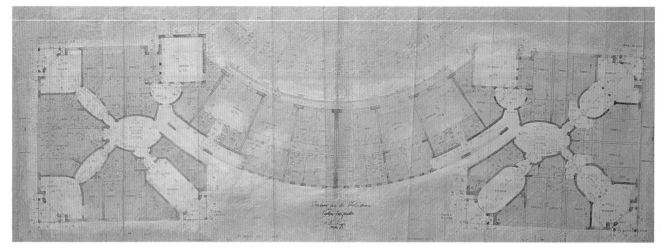

FROM ABOVE: PLAN OF THE CRESCENT; VIEW OF THE CRESCENT FROM THE STREET

FROM ABOVE: SKETCH STUDY OF PLAN AND ELEVATION FOR THE CRESCENT; VIEW OF THE CRESCENT BUILDING WITH THE FLANKING TOWERS FACING THE GREEN

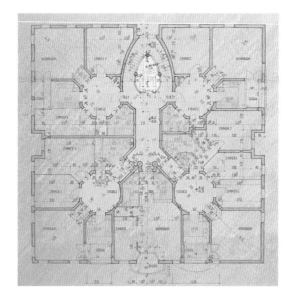

FROM ABOVE: KRIER HOUSE PLAN; VIEW TOWARDS THE KRIER HOUSE

FROM ABOVE: VIEW DOWN THE GREEN TOWARDS THE CRESCENT; DETAIL OF THE KRIER HOUSE

VIA TRIUMPHALIS
KARLSRUHE, 1979

The point of this investigation was to produce outline proposals responding to a broad range of urban planning issues, from paving to building facades. The Karlsruhe authorities were looking not for definitive solutions, but for fresh ideas from someone new to the area, in order to stimulate discussion about the goals and methods of urban planning in the city. The starting point for the project was the idea of setting up the Via Triumphalis much as it was originally, with greens and squares bordering onto it, and a highly defined square at the primary intersection. An honorific causeway is thus restored between the castle of Karlsruhe and the landscaped gardens at the south end of the site. The urban fabric and natural green space interact as equal partners in a dialogue between solid and void. In place of the old Neoclassical gateway by Weinbrenner with its radiating routes into the southern parts of the city we now have a section of the Autobahn. I suggest building the little square above this irreparable existing anti-city nightmare to create a pleasant space for pedestrians.

FROM ABOVE L TO R: EXISTING SITE PLAN; AERIAL VIEW WITH THE TRAIN STATION AND ZOO IN THE FOREGROUND AND CASTLE IN THE DISTANCE; PROPOSED SITE PLAN; THE MARKET-PLACE LOOKING TOWARDS THE CASTLE

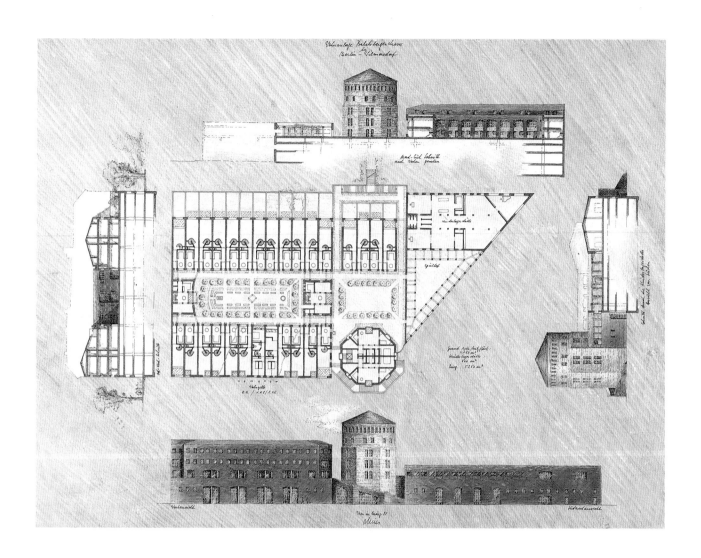

HOUSING IN BABELSBERGERSTRASSE
WILMERSDORF, 1981

This housing development is placed on top of an existing two-storey industrial building. My concern has been to alter the random arrangement of the complex so that the triangular playground of the kindergarten, a source of unrestrained noise, is separated from the main garden area for the housing by courtyards containing workshops and studios. The new building is limited in plan types by the need to follow the axis of the existing structure. The corner tower stands in line with and visually terminates an adjoining street. It contains a deck accessible by a large, open staircase. This tower is, in effect the focal point of the site, rising two storeys above the rest of the project and being treated as a solid figural object. It is bordered by an equivalent open space which acts as organiser for the units and leads on one side into a triangular columned court and on the other into a long landscaped green with a *crescent at the far end acting as a terminator. More than half of the residential units look onto private gardens or yards at the back of the site. The project is conceived almost as an 'acropolis' or elevated complex of houses and courts hinging on the polygonal tower which defines the obtuse corner of the site. In its spatial complexity a richness of form is secured for the enjoyment of the residents who in crossing from one side of the complex to the other experience a variety of architectural relationships. These relationships distinguish one grouping of units from the other yet tie them together at the same time through the system of interconnected passages and gates. The facades at the street level have large, well lit openings, which become smaller and more regular on the upper floors. The project is thus tied together both spatially and through the consistency of the architectural vocabulary.*

PLAN, SECTION AND ELEVATIONS OF THE PROPOSAL

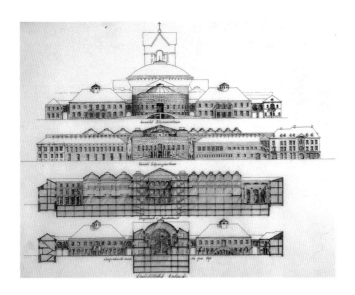

STATE LIBRARY
KARLSRUHE, 1979

The geometry and form of the new library – particularly its courtyard elevation – are largely determined by the important existing buildings on the site, which will be retained and carefully incorporated into the new scheme.

I believe it is important to create a complete, closed facade opposite Weinbrenner's St Stephen's Church. To achieve this, it will be necessary to modify the facades of the townhouses adjoining the complex. The main entry is orientated towards the portico of St Stephen: the colonnade of the church is echoed in the stelae of a gentle ramp. The square itself remains open to traffic; only the area between the library entrance and the church portico is specially marked by paving. The buildings do not compete with each other in terms of mass.

My proposal develops Weinbrenner's second design for the church, with its provision for auxiliary public buildings and an ordered landscaping. The entrance facade continues the existing facade with the sole interruption of the entrance portico with its octagonal skylight, while the Blumenstrasse facade is intentionally broken down into object-buildings framed on either side by extensions of the two other street elevations.

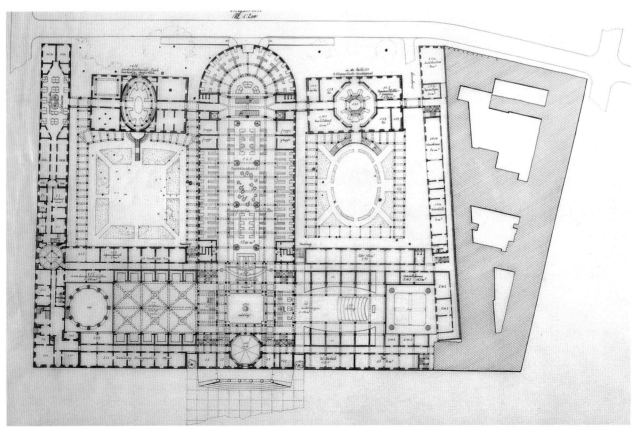

OPPOSITE: PROJECT DEVELOPMENT SKETCHES, STATE LIBRARY, KARLSRUHE; *FROM ABOVE:* ELEVATONS AND SECTIONS; GROUND FLOOR PLAN

HOUSING IN KURFÜRSTENDAMM
BERLIN, 1981

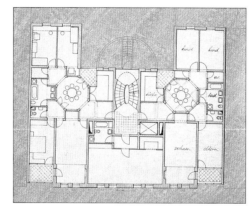

This project is an attempt to mediate in a decent manner between the so-called 'marble house' and a fine sandstone facade dating from the end of last century. The competition was won by a commercial planning office in Hamburg, with a low-rent post-modern scheme. This being essentially a facade exercise, the building sets up a glazed background against which to place the central element which includes a gabled roof. The attic storey is further empha-sised by a row of round openings which sit above a balcony that runs the length of the facade. The first, second and third floors are lit by a successively larger number of windows which thereby add lightness and make a transition to the glazed balcony. The isolated part of the facade echoes the proportions of the existing buildings on the street and by pushing away from the rest of the building allows it to rise unobtru-sively above the street roofscape.

FROM ABOVE: ELEVATION; PLAN SHOWING THE ADJACENT UNITS; VIEW OF THE PROJECT WITH THE RUINS OF KAISER FRIEDRICH WILHELM'S MEMORIAL CHURCH ON THE LEFT

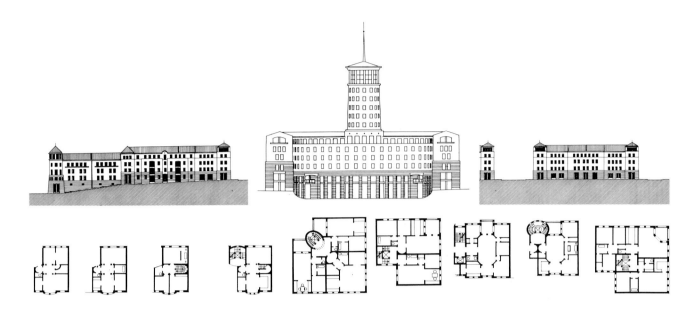

PLACE DE L'ETOILE
LUXEMBOURG, 1982

The Place de l'Etoile is the site of the border path that used to run in front of the fortifications of Luxembourg. Today it still gives a true sense of entry to the city. Arriving from Arlon in Belgium in the west, you face first a steep descent and then a climb back up to the city. My project proposed placing a new facade on the square, which is in the form of a half-circle. My point of reference was the famous 'Neue Brücke' which links the area around the station with the centre of the city. Throughout the project the elevations are given rusticated bases

and regular openings; blocks being ended by corner towers as is often the case in the old city of Luxembourg. These towers are echoed on a grander scale by a large tower that projects from the crescent building. In a manner not unlike the Admiralty Arch in London, the crescent is punctured by two roads which converge at this point. The streets and boulevards regularise the existing urban fabric. The housing units are varied in size and typology, but are generally arranged around a central room accessed by a spacious stair tower.

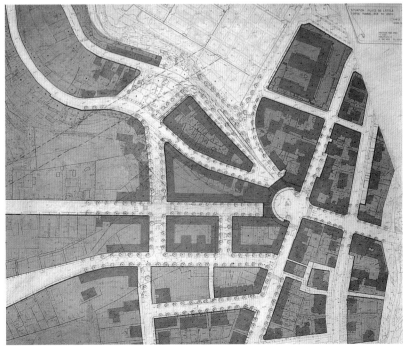

FROM ABOVE: PLANS AND ELEVATIONS OF THE PROPOSAL; SKETCH OF THE SEMI-CIRCULAR SQUARE; SITE PLAN

HOUSING IN BREITENFURTERSTRASSE
VIENNA, 1981-87

The construction of a residential complex in the outskirts of Vienna implies the clear intention of combining an autochthonous architectural language with the functional requirements of a residential space. It is necessary to contemplate its connections with the surroundings as much in terms of communications with the city centre as with the accidents of typography and the pre-existing components. The arrangement of the various units of construction is defined by the conditioning factors of the terrain and the need to create a physical and aesthetic inter-relationship. Starting from certain time-honoured postulates, I organised the volumes in a classical manner in tone with an up-to-date treatment in pursuit of an improvement in the quality of life. The project is a part of the general renewal of the social environment of Vienna, which dates back to the beginning of the 80s. Various competitions were organised in which opposing solutions were proposed; both the contribution of Richter and Gerngrob, with their surprising innovative vision, and the residential complex by myself, Wachberger and Gebhart are based on traditional classical concepts. The aesthetic suggestions are indicated by the natural and architectural surroundings: the detached houses, inns and green intertwine to form an autochthonous landscape into which the new project must fit harmoniously to the benefit of the residents of Breitenfurterstrasse.

OPPOSITE: PLANS, SECTIONS AND ELEVATIONS OF THE BUILDING; *FROM ABOVE L TO R:* MODEL OF ENTIRE COMPLEX; SKETCH STUDY OF THE TOWER AT THE END OF THE TRIANGULAR BLOCK; SKETCH STUDY OF THE ROUND COURT; *OVERLEAF:* CAMILLO-SITTE PLATZ

FROM ABOVE: SOUTH FACADE OF PROJECT END-PIECE; SOUTH PORTICO, CAMILLO-SITTE PLATZ; *OPPOSITE:* THE SCULPTURE PLACED IN THE CENTRE OF CAMILLO-SITTE PLATZ

ACADEMY OF FINE ARTS
BERLIN, 1983

The task here was to plug a gap in the Lützenburgerstraße. As in previous projects, I aimed to fit the new construction seamlessly into the existing fabric. The building's function and pedagogic character are expressed symbolically in a gigantic relief around the plinth and in two monumental figures designed by Johannes Grützke, while the building's typology and internal spatial composition attempt to reflect the high standards that are justifiably expected of an academy of fine arts. The project hinges around an amphitheatrical foyer which is approached through a long open court. Two large sculptures which reduce the monumental scale of the arched entrance opening. The street elevation is treated with rusticated bands interrupted at various levels by string courses, the whole being treated as a continuation of the surrounding fabric. The rear facade is interrupted by a deep recess meant to pull the visitor into the building via a columned archway.

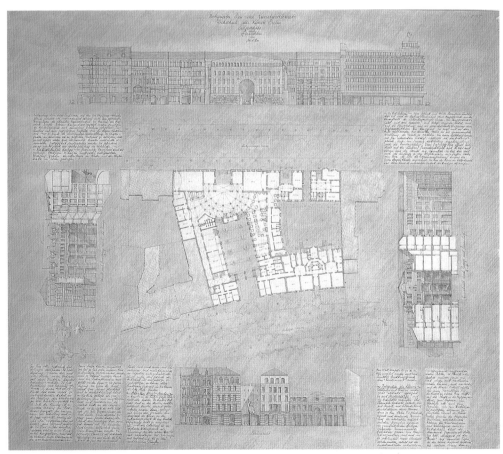

OPPOSITE, FROM ABOVE: BAS-RELIEF FROM THE BASE OF THE MAIN FACADE BY JOHANNES GRÜTZKE; STREET VIEW; *FROM ABOVE:* BAS-RELIEF FROM THE BASE OF THE MAIN FACADE BY JOHANNES GRÜTZKE; ELEVATIONS AND PLANS OF THE PROJECT

KRIER FLAT
VIENNA, 1980-84

Working for myself, I was able to give the typology that I had first tried out in the Schinkelplatz in Berlin a more generous, spatially rich development. I could not resist the challenge of trying to organise as many room types as possible into an exciting sequence. The small-scale composition allowed a greater range of rooms than can be read from the plan alone. The sense of transparency and the alternation of ceiling heights create surprising illusions and plays of light which change with the passing seasons.

For the first time, the development of space out of a geometrically ordered plan touched my private life and changed my work. I've given myself up to it – I'm happy at home. Throughout, the flat space is treated figurally, each room being rendered plastically in both plan and section. The centrally located living room is crowned by a tall cupola with clerestory fenestration. In moving through the house one has the sense of a 'promenade architecturelle', each space leading to new discoveries. When seen from the roof, the flat transforms from a series of spaces into a neat collection of volumes, all offering generous natural light to the interior.

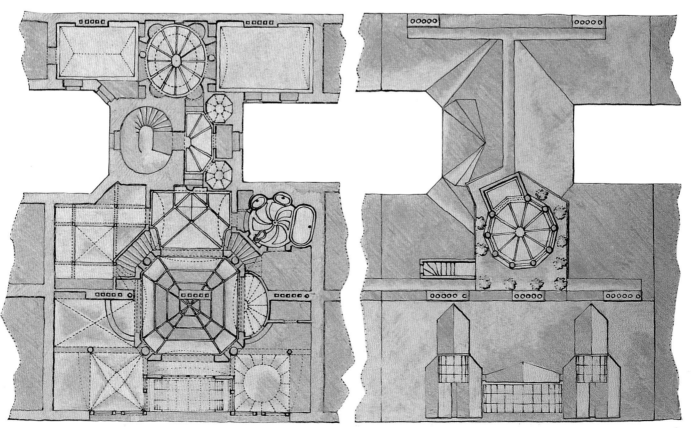

OPPOSITE, FROM ABOVE: VIEW OF THE KITCHEN; THE LIVING ROOM; *FROM ABOVE L TO R:* ELEVATION; SECTION; FLOOR PLAN; ROOF PLAN

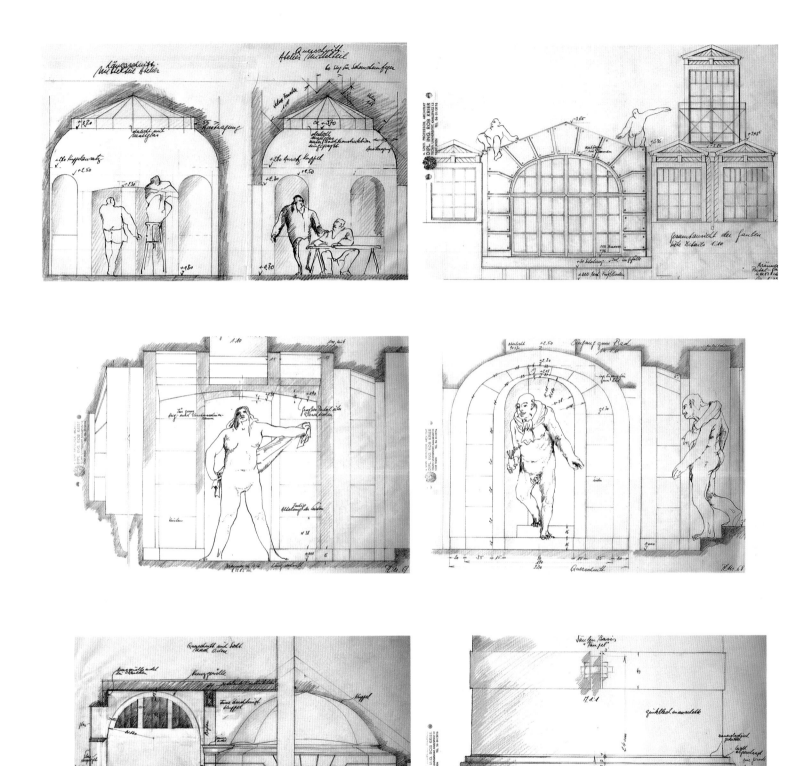

OPPOSITE: VIEW OF THE BATHROOM; *ABOVE:* WORKING DRAWINGS

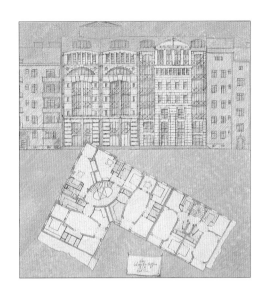

HOUSING IN SCHRANKENBERGGASSE
VIENNA, 1983-86

This asymmetrical corner site contains two buildings which are meant to appear to have been designed independently of each other. The corner building, containing the largest flats, has two roughly symmetrical elevations, each with two bays. The main living rooms are elongated octagons oriented to receive light from two directions; the south sun is captured in the green central courtyard. The smaller building is also for the most part oriented towards a peaceful courtyard. Both buildings are designed to receive as much natural light as possible. The unit types are based on an atrium arrangement with central stairwells. Though different in their overall facade composition, both buildings have a rusticated base and symmetrically arranged openings. The facades facing the courtyard are divided into sections comprising two units in plan, linked by arched openings with a dividing wall. Thermal windows on the street elevations are echoed on the upper storeys. The main entrance of the corner building is marked by a Doric column surmounted by a bronze sculpture.

OPPOSITE: VIEW OF THE CORNER BUILDING; *ABOVE:* ELEVATIONS AND PLAN OF THE BUILDINGS;
BELOW: SKETCH OF ENTRY WITH SCULPTURAL GROUP

An der Hirschstettenstraße in Wien   ... aß Alle 11.8.83 rol. teie

Dieser Gassenabschnitt baue ich mit meinen ehemaligen + jetzigen Mitarbeitern
und Architekten: Haus 1 Kies, Haus 2 Stelzhammer, Haus 3 Gangusch,
Haus 4 Böhm, Haus 5 Cufer, Haus 6 Schauer, Häuser 7–10 Kies,
Haus 11 Kräftner, Haus 12 Steiner, Haus 13 Jentlin, Haus 14 Fellner.

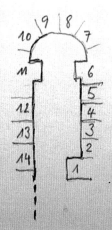

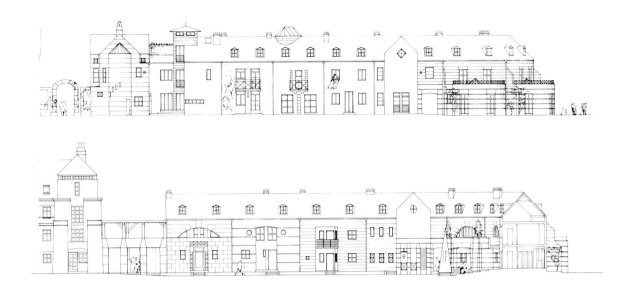

HOUSING IN HIRSCHSTETTEN
VIENNA, 1983

I divided this commission for 14 single-family row houses amongst my colleagues and assistants in the hope of creating a textbook example of my philosophy of small-scale urban planning. Unfortunately it became an illustration of just what can go wrong when an architect is not able to supervise the site. Our designs were crudely changed during construction to the point where we felt we could no longer identify fully with the project. We were cheated out of three years'

work which, nevertheless, we hoped would still have a didactic purpose in the executed drawings and plans.

My co-workers on the scheme were Walter Stelzhammer, Kunibert Gangusch, Stefan Böhm, Gretl Cufer and Ute Schauer. On separate parts of the project the following collaborated: Johann Kräftner, Dietmar Steiner, Franz Demblin, Gerhard Fellner. I designed the two ends of the street, always in keeping with the local urban character.

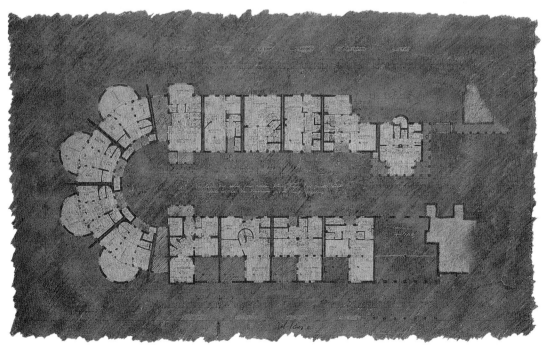

OPPOSITE: STREET SCENE; *FROM ABOVE:* ELEVATIONS; THE SMALL SQUARE (DIAMETER 13.40M); PLAN OF THE PROJECT

PARVIS N.D. À AMIENS

84

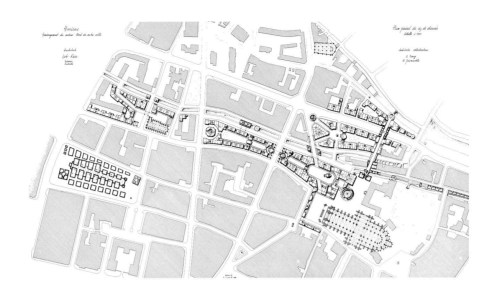

RECONSTRUCTION OF THE CITY CENTRE
AMIENS 1984-91

The initial idea of the plan is simple: to erase the memory of war-time destruction by creating a new urban tissue similar to the original one and in the same location. Three main points serve this basic assumption: the scale of the old city; relationship of its public spaces; and traditional typology of the local buildings and their combination. These ideas were my response to the competition launched by the city in 1984. Unlike a purely architectural plan dealing with quantity alone, the plan includes the archi-

tectural and urbanistic disciplines: creation of the South-North Axis linking the Parvis to the Saint-Leu Neighbourhood. The project comprises an urban tissue structured with very dense streets and squares linking the Parvis to the Bas-Parvis and the northern neighbourhood. The scheme proposes to create new alignments of trees and to fill inner courtyards with trees and plants. By setting up a series of squares and courts linked in the traditional manner, this part of the city will regain its sense of place and community spirit.

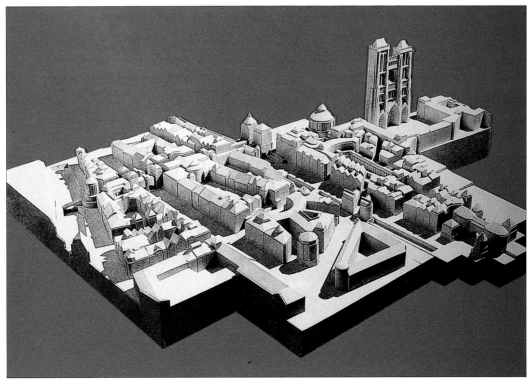

OPPOSITE: THE NEW SQUARE, NOTRE DAME; *FROM ABOVE:* PLAN OF THE COMPETITION PROJECT;
CATHEDRAL AND SURROUNDINGS AFTER THE BOMBARDMENTS IN 1941; MODEL OF THE QUARTERS SURROUNDING THE CATHEDRAL

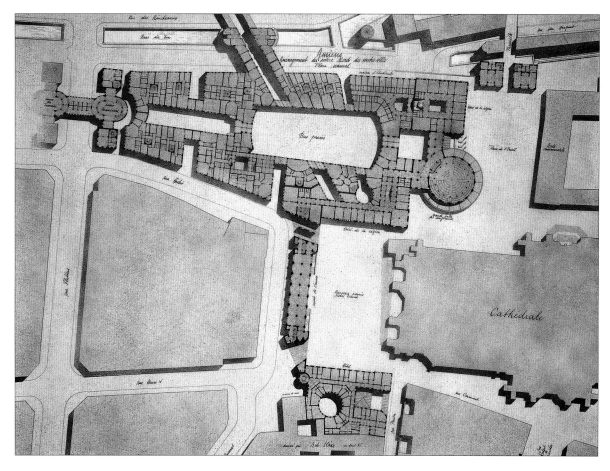

FROM ABOVE L TO R: PLAN SHOWING THE PLACE DE NOTRE DAME IN FRONT OF THE CATHEDRAL; RIVER VIEW; PONTE VECCHIO; PLACE EDOUARD DAVID; BAS-PARVIS; HOUSING ON THE BRAS DES TANNEURS; NEW MARKET HALL

FROM ABOVE: CURRENT PLAN SHOWING THE CONTINUITY OF THE HISTORICAL URBAN FABRIC;
AXONOMETRIC OF THE AREA AROUND THE CATHEDRAL WITH THE LAW FACULTY, UNIVERSITY LIBRARY AND OTHER UNIVERSITY BUILDINGS

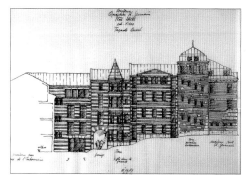 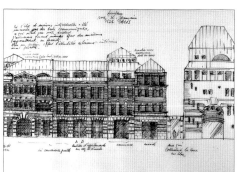 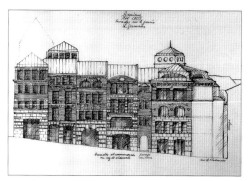

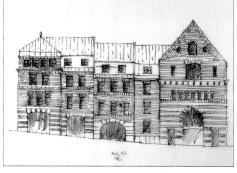 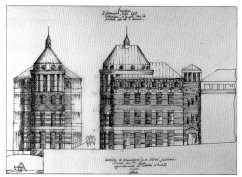 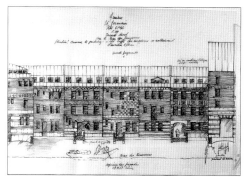

FROM ABOVE: SQUARE IN FRONT OF THE CHURCH OF ST GERMAIN; URBAN FACADE ADJUSTMENTS IN THE ST GERMAIN QUARTER

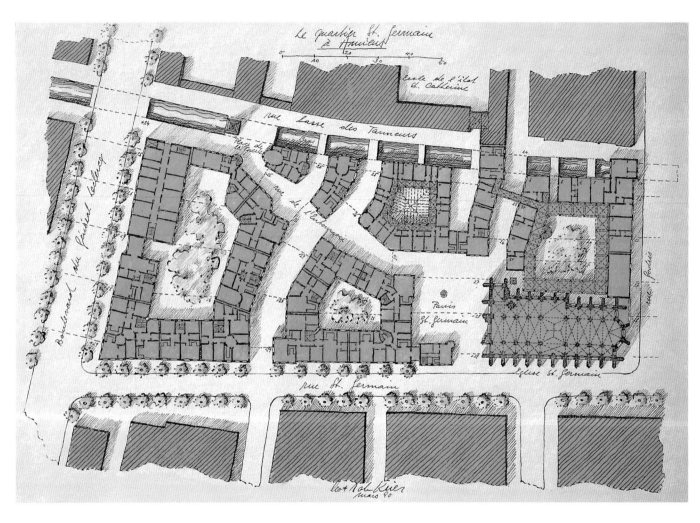

FROM ABOVE: PLAN OF A QUARTER SHOWING RESIDENTIAL SUBDIVISIONS; MODEL OF THE SAME QUARTER DESIGNED AND BUILT BY KRIER STUDENTS

URBAN PROPOSAL FOR THE FORELLENWEG
SALZBURG, 1983-84

Four hundred flats are equivalent in size to a small town – a factor reflected in the place-making typology of this project. The scheme is designed to allow a high degree of spatial complexity within only 10 blocks, in contrast to the alienating uniformity of much current planning. The layout was determined by a desire to fit in with the surrounding environment. All blocks allow a degree of transparency, and include passages which link the courtyards to each other, encouraging social interaction amongst both children and adults.

All the streets lead to a central square, which has a strong sense of enclosure. The required communal facilities are not scattered throughout the complex but placed together in buildings of a monumental character. This creates the kind of spaces for ritual, cultural, political and social occasions which I believe are an essential component of any true community. Such buildings have always formed the nucleus of every urban agglomeration. If they are not there, the place is only a settlement – a precursor of an urban culture.

OPPOSITE, FROM ABOVE: VIEW DOWN A SIDE STREET; AXONOMETRIC OF THE PROJECT; *FROM ABOVE:* CORNER TOWERS; PLAN OF PROJECT

OPPOSITE: AXONOMETRIC PLAN AND VIEWS OF THE PROJECT; *FROM ABOVE:* THE OVAL SQUARE; THE OCTAGONAL COURTYARD

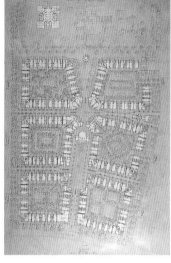

URBAN PLAN FOR LIESING
VIENNA, 1985

The Liesing project picks up the basic concept of my early scheme for Aalter (1966), consisting of extremely simple row houses which can be oriented in any direction, with parking in the courtyards. The central area contains a complex interconnecting composition of public squares, which form the backbone of the neighbourhood. There are provisions for full public and commercial facilities. The plan is essentially symmetrical with a long green connecting on to an enclosed octagonal square which leads out onto an open landscaped park. At one end of the long green is a circular Culture Pavilion which is echoed inversely by a crescent immediately behind it. The site splays out gradually, becoming wider at the park end, yet providing an essentially equal proportion of open space to each block. These spaces are filled with trees and vegetation providing the residential units with a welcome contrast to the continuous streetscape to which their entrance facades belong. The variety of space sets up a dialogue with the symmetry of the site plan, the residential courts linking back to the central spine of the enclosed greens which are perceived as walled gardens to discover and explore.

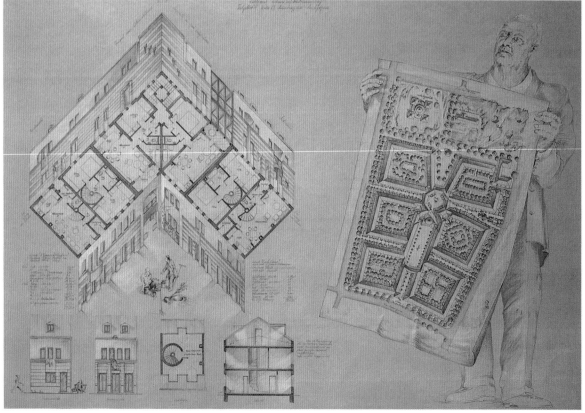

FROM ABOVE L TO R: THE CULTURE PAVILION; PLAN; AERIAL VIEW OF THE ENCLOSED GREENS; DETAIL OF TYPICAL UNIT PLANS

    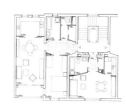 

HOUSING CLOSE TO THE REICHSBRÜCKE
VIENNA, 1985

The project is comprised of two large courtyards joined at the centre by a of free-standing market building, pavilion and kindergarten. The urban fabric of the historic centre of Vienna is maintained as are the formal characteristics, particularly the interplay between object and street facade.

Each court acts as a distinct gathering place defined by landscaping elements and a different feeling of enclosure. The sense of community in each courtyard is intended to contrast with the open public space to the south of the project which is defined by continuous rows of trees much like boulevards in

the existing urban fabric of Vienna. Each house type is a variation of the atrium plan with rooms arranged around a central space. Within each unit a spacious staircase provides independent access to the upper floors while overlooking public spaces. The street elevations preserve the traditional street frontage and are sub-divided into separate blocks with rusticated bases, central elements with large openings, and upper attic zones which provide a reading of solidity. The facades relate to each other in their formal characteristics and architectural details.

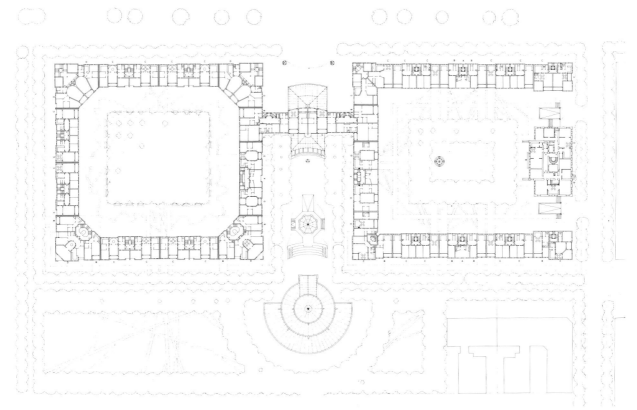

FROM ABOVE L TO R: STREET VIEW; RESIDENTIAL UNIT PLANS; VIEW OF MEXICOPLATZ; PLAN OF THE PROJECT

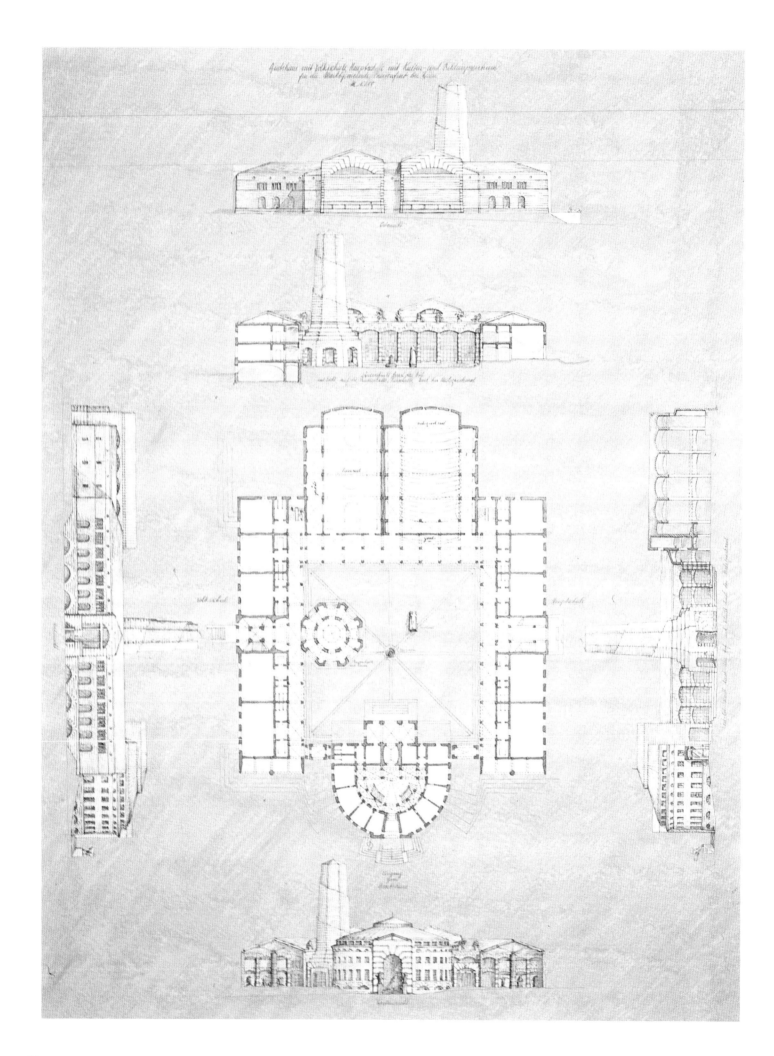

96

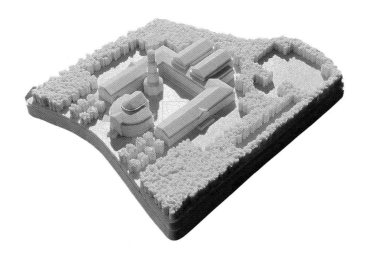

CULTURAL CENTRE IN BREITENFURT
VIENNA, 1985

Breitenfurt, near Vienna, is a scattered village without a focal point – not even a church. Moved by indignation at this poor state of affairs, I made this school complex particularly ceremonial, in the manner of an abbey, which can give form to a place. My intention was to create a true centre that would attract people towards it, including, naturally, the young people who study there. A large court or square surrounded by arcades is bordered by public buildings and an amphitheatrical hall which protrudes into the open space. A tall, free-standing tower occupies one side of the square, breaking the strict axial symmetry of the project in a way reminiscent to a Hellenistic agora, the Asklepeion at Pergamon for example, which was the result of architectural accretion over the years. The ceremo-nial qualities of the project are thus offset by the relaxed juxtaposition of formal elements. The tower's unique shape, with its spiralling body, stands out over the rest of the building enticing the visitor into the square in order to view the entire structure against the arcade court facades. Rustication plays an important part in the facade compositions, imbuing the building with a sense of solidity as is the case often with abbeys and monastic structures. The solidity of the elevations, the tranquility of the arcaded square, and ceremonial qualities of the architectural composition unite to create a unique place for an otherwise soul-less village. Here at last is a concept for creating a heart, or communal gathering space in Breitenfurt, as should be the case in all human settlements.

OPPOSITE: PLAN AND ELEVATIONS OF THE PROJECT; *FROM ABOVE:* MODEL VIEW; SKETCH VIEWS OF THE PROJECT

BELVEDERE
FREIBURG, 1985-86

The pavilion is conceived as a tholos *building or free-standing baldacchino meant to act as a focal point in its urban surroundings. The columns that support the massive dome, or cupola, are meant to appear especially solid and for this reason they are not much taller proportionally to the roofing structure. A continuous band of* clathrae *just below the pavilion eaves makes the building more horizontal in appearance, and provides a historical reference to the Greco-Roman typology from which it springs.*

A combination of solid stone and metal architectural elements set up an interesting dialogue of materials and scales, giving the building a richness that contrasts with the simple volumetric shape. The stairs to the upper dome wrap asymmetrically around an octagonal core. The construction has a massive base, but dissolves as it rises upwards. The form of the octagon is accentuated on the first floor by powerful round columns, above which are set 16 slender supports for the dome and its central top light.

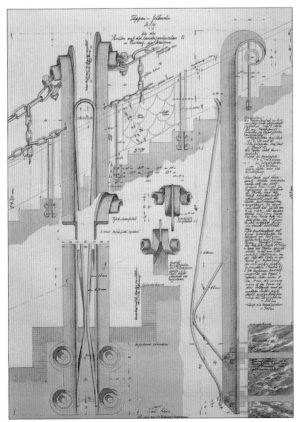 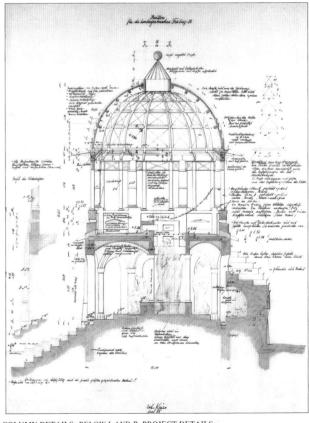

OPPOSITE: THE PAVILION AS BUILT; *ABOVE:* BASE AND COLUMN DETAILS; *BELOW L AND R:* PROJECT DETAILS;
OVERLEAF L TO R: WORKING PLANS OF THE TWO LEVELS; DETAIL PLAN AND ELEVATION OF THE PAVILION COLUMNS

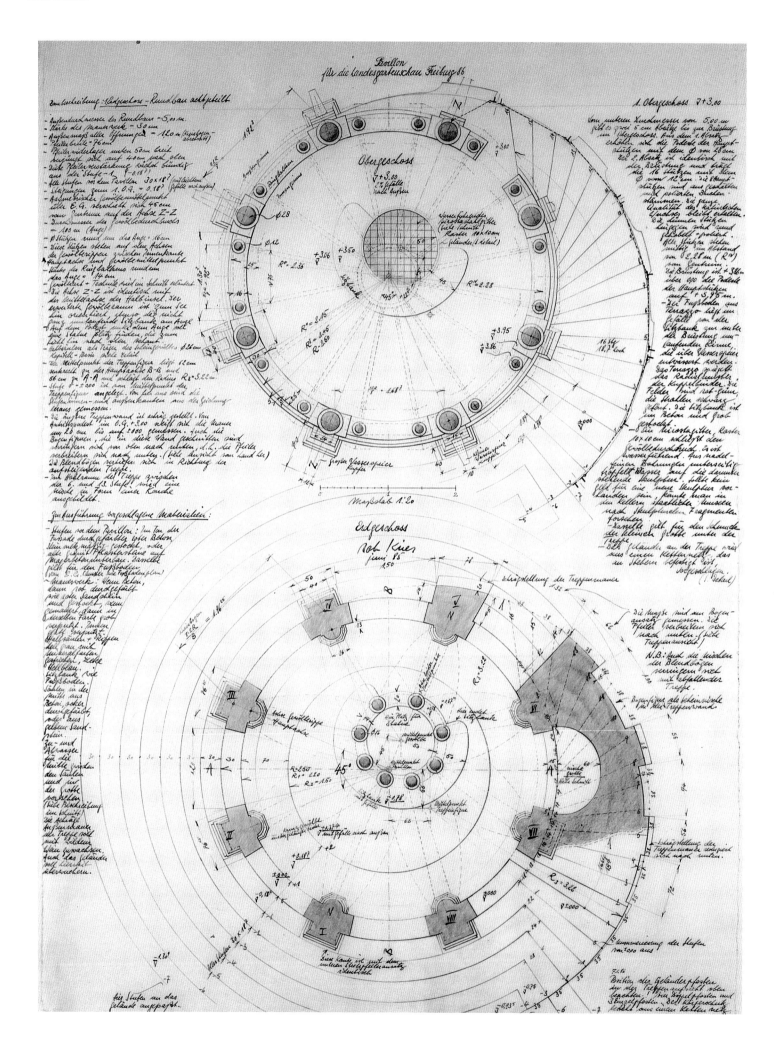

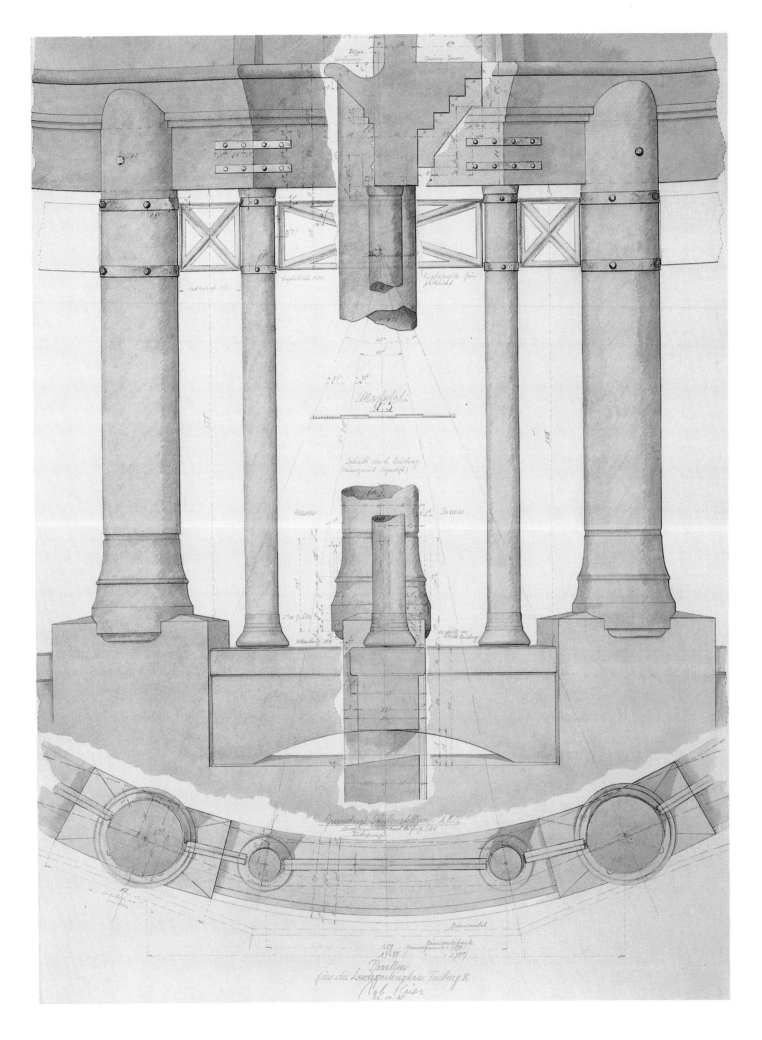

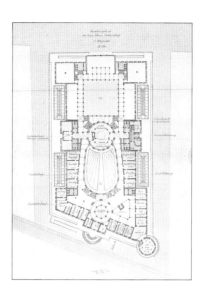

OFFICE BUILDING
KLOSTERNEUBURG, VIENNA, 1986

I generally never have any luck when I compete against friends. This competition, which also attracted Heinz Tesar and Adolf Krischanitz, was no exception. My proposal was too ceremonial, too showy for the leading chain of department stores in the country. Tesar won, his project was built, and proved a great success.

I wanted to base the complex on the typology of a traditional Lower Austrian courtyard building. I used as my model the Klosterneuburg monastery, of which unfortunately only a fragment survives today. The project comprises an axially arranged series of courts and atria around which the smaller rooms are grouped. At the heart of the scheme is a circular exhibition building which connects on one side to an oval

outdoor court; on the other side to a rectangular cloister. The acute corner of the site is marked by the round Director's Tower which acts as a hinge, linking the entrance facade to the longer side of the project. The entrance itself is placed at the top of a monumental stair built into a heavy rusticated base surmounted by pergolas. The arched doorway looms dramatically over the stair, which is echoed on the rear elevation on either side of a similar portal. In plan the building sets up a dialogue between the larger figural spaces and the smaller rooms which face out onto the streets and make up the plain surfaces which continue the traditional street facades. Pronounced string courses divide the elevations and provide them with an attic storey which crowns the entire project.

FROM ABOVE L TO R: PLAN OF THE PROJECT; CONFERENCE AND EXHIBITION HALL; COURT WITH THE EXHIBITION HALL

MÖNCHSTEIN HOTEL EXTENSION
SALZBURG, 1986-87

An incredibly beautiful site over Salzburg in the Mönch mountains is the setting for an existing picturesque castle haunted by a cultured lover of art who was at once delighted with our proposal for extending the building's hotel accommodation. We did this by setting up a court closed on one side by the castle walls, with a ceremonial entrance and generous openings overlooking the landscape. The architecture does not compete with that of the castle, taking on as it does a different, if related, vocabulary of elements. Subtle references to crenellated walls are made by emphasising the brackets of one tower. The rich interplay of volumes in the castle inspired the complex juxtapositions of the new elevations, which seek in their own way to set up a picturesque composition, equal to but not competitive with the older structure. The building is at once extroverted as it is introverted – the court allowing dramatic views and glimpses of the castle and the large opening on the exterior facades setting up breathtaking vistas of the forested landscape. The old and new structure meet at different elevations and do not therefore run the risk of appearing to be one structure but rather read together as separate but linked entities each built in different periods yet embodying the very same fascination with the site and desire to relate, self-consciously, to nature. The new forms are meant to be reminiscent of the cliff surfaces surrounding the site.*

FROM ABOVE L TO R: PLANS AND SECTIONS; WEST FACADE; NORTH FACADE

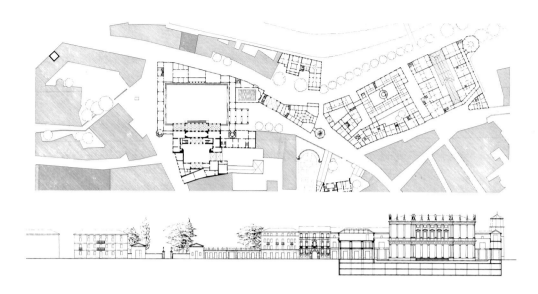

REMODELLING OF THE PIAZZALE MATTEOTTI
VICENZA, 1986

When Palladio built the Palazzo Chiericati it lay on the edge of the town. The main facade, which now overlooks the piazza, was originally planned to look onto a garden. At present, the palazzo's relationship to its urban surroundings is quite clearly unresolved. The main idea of the plan was to rectify this situation and at last reconcile the palazzo with its urban surroundings. The scheme takes its form and scale from the square in front of Palladio's basilica in the centre of the town.

After a close analysis and evaluation of the built fabric of the Piazzale Matteotti each new insertion was carefully designed

to maintain a compositional dialogue with the existing buildings. My freehand sketches give a better idea of the nature of the urban environment we were trying to create. Some of my Italian colleagues might find it frivolous for a Northern European to adopt such a radical approach to the fabric of one of their cities. In my defence, I would like to say that Italy has had just as much difficulty as other European countries in dealing with its historic building fabric. Some room for innovation must exist, otherwise the living art of urban architecture will degenerate into pure conservation.

FROM ABOVE L TO R: PLAN SHOWING URBAN CONTEXT; ELEVATON OF PROJECT WITH THE PALAZZO CHIERICATI; PROJECT ELEVATONS; VIEW TOWARDS PALAZZO CHIERICATI FROM PIAZZALE MATTEOTTI; ROAD LEADING INTO PIAZZALE MATTEOTTI

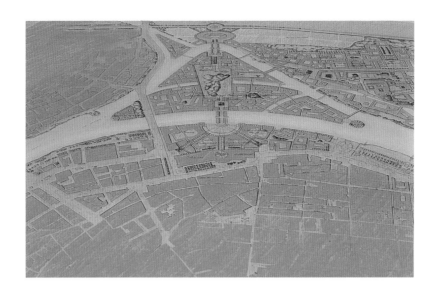

SEVILLE WORLD EXPO 92
SPAIN, 1986

In the spirit of past International Exhibitions, my plan envisaged that this singular event would create something of lasting value for the city. I proposed a succinct link between the Expo buildings, the Carthusian monastery, and the old town. The intention was that the whole neighbourhood should continue to contribute to the city. The pavilion buildings are placed behind the monastery. They enclose a gigantic park, which becomes even larger after the exhibition is dismantled. The confluence of the rivers and the triangular island to the east of the Expo park become a node by which the site can be approached from the city of Seville. The park is tear-drop shaped and ended by the stadium, approached axially across the landscaped space. The pavilions are visited by means of a skylit avenue along which are located small courts and squares. A real streetscape is thereby created, protected from the elements, from which visitors can reach the exhibits. Along the length of the avenue views are afforded into the park by means of regularly spaced perpendicular streets which create what is in essence a regularised urban grid. The sweep of the pavilions and central avenue gives the plan a dynamic character contrasting with the tranquil setting of the monastery and the city.

FROM ABOVE L TO R: AERIAL VIEW OF PLAN; SITE PLAN; ENTRANCE TO EXPO GROUNDS; THE BRICK PAVILIONS

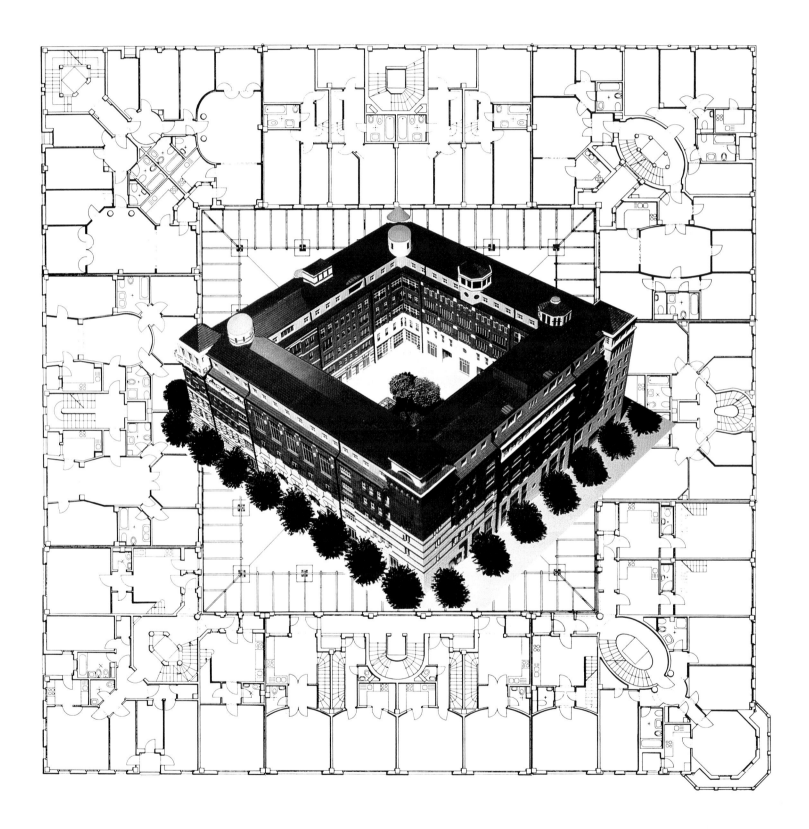

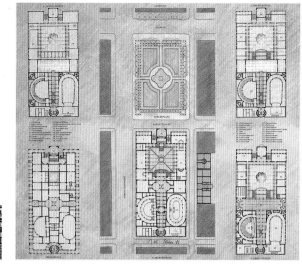

TOWN HALL
MANNHEIM, 1986

During the 17th century a strange building type appeared in Mannheim – a pair of structures, often differing in function and style, linked in the middle by a tower. The first example was the Reformed Church. After that came the Concordia Church and attached school; the old town hall and the Church of St Sebastian; and finally, at the beginning of the 18th century, a commodity house, which later became the new town hall. The tone of my proposal is evocative of the town hall tower, a Baroque jewel which survived the ravages of war only to be destroyed in a 1960s act of vandalism. The perspective view and elevations show the two facade units of the town hall linked by a central tower facing the square. A skylit amphitheatrical auditorium and hall are the main feature of the interior, maximising the use of natural light. The symmetry of the composition is broken by the different room typologies on either side of the glass-vaulted hall which leads into the main space. This is a rectangular interior court, in all senses a piazza meant to be used as a gathering place. Through the glass roof over this space, the tower facing the square is clearly visible linking the interior and exterior of the building.

FROM ABOVE L TO R: TOWN HALL ELEVATIONS; FLOOR PLANS; SKETCH PERSPECTIVE OF THE PROPOSED BUILDINGS

RESORT TOWN
SISTIANA, TRIESTE, 1987

Close to the place where Rilke penned his Duino Elegies, this is without doubt the most beautiful unspoilt bay on the Adriatic coast. A massive wall of cliffs drops into the sea and when the stormy Bora begins to blow it is almost impossible to stand upright. A breathtaking site! We attempted to break up the complex and set it in niches in the cliffs, to avoid damaging the landscape. This gave rise to a three-part scheme: an urban harbour at the foot of the dramatic cliffs, with a spa centre nestling amongst the greenery a little way above it, and at the top a mountain village, clinging to the slopes of an old quarry. The town is linked to the larger harbour along a broadwalk and corniche which hugs the waterfront. Upon entering the site the marina is heralded by a lighthouse tower which separates the built area from a wedge-shaped inlet. Bridges link the town to a small island, giving the site an almost Venetian air. The houses are arranged casually around winding roads behind the marina's regularised facades and crescent-shaped end. Seen from the water, the massive cliffs overlooking the project appear to complete the sense of enclosure set-up by the horse-shoe shaped marina. The natural rock drops away in the direction of the harbour and a winding road leads through the hills back toward the mountain village with views out over the far side of the peninsula. Rather than occupy the site, the project tries to enhance its particular nature.

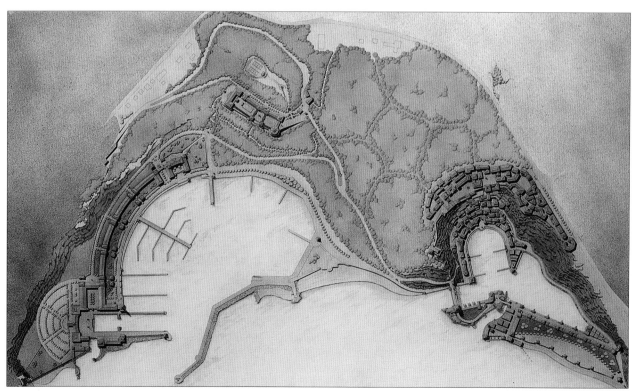

OPPOSITE, FROM ABOVE L TO R: THE CURVED CORNICHE; BUTTRESSED TOWER; CENTRAL SQUARE; STREET SCENE; *FROM ABOVE:* THE PROJECT IN ITS NATURAL CONTEXT; SITE PLAN

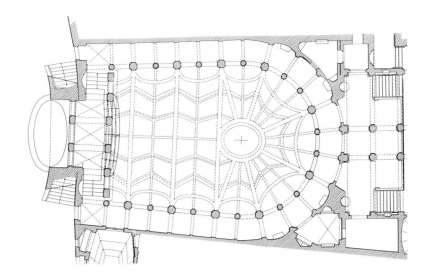

PARISH HALL
PORDENONE, VENETO, 1986-88

The building had to be inserted into the courtyard of a historic complex, which gave rise to certain irregularities in the plan. It also suffered from cost savings made when it went on site.

I chose a form of vault with a ribbed structure for maximum transparency and light as the topography of the site restricted the spatial development of the hall. The horseshoe shape of the hall is traced out by a pergola on the roof garden above, which occupies the former monastery courtyard. The garden is linked with the lower street level by an open double staircase crowned with a glazed pavilion. There is a fountain at the bottom of the stairs, but some of the figures which were to adorn it remain unmade. An end building in the courtyard had become structurally unsound and was given a new form. A clerestory band of round windows wraps the interior of the hall

and a continuous ambulatory allows access from the main entrance to the back of the project without disrupting the activities in the hall. A circular lantern occupies the centre of the vault above the altar, bringing the focus to the geometric heart of the space. Rectangular pillars alternating with pairs of columns create a distinct rhythm in the ambulatory which is further emphasised by the subdivisions of the vault ribs. In general, a tripartite arrangement has been used with three openings between each pillar and three circular clerestory windows directly above these. The low vault of the hall is given a sense of height by means of the pillars and clerestory windows, as well as the circular oculus which is intended to mark the position of an altar.

OPPOSITE: VIEW OF THE GRAND STAIR; *FROM ABOVE:* GROUND FLOOR PLAN; PARISH HALL IN THE PROCESS OF BEING COMPLETED

OLD PEOPLE'S HOUSING
MULHEIM AN DER RUHR, DUSSELDORF, 1988-93

One dislikes to speak of old people's homes, which more often than not are ghettos for people in need of care. However it is a bitter necessity in our society and one which is rapidly increasing. Church institutions and private groups are more able to organise this important social work in a humane way than the public institutions.

I followed the model of a Beguin complex in which elderly couples live in their own small house with a garden which is connected to other such units as well as workshops, care centres, a library, a coffee house, doctor's offices, a small therapy room and a chapel. The individual houses are connected by means of a care-corridor to the complex's other functions, so that in cases of emergency elderly people can be pushed in their own bed to the care station.

It is to the merit of the Berlin architects von Herder and Fedderson to have brought together five other colleagues and to have allowed each one of them to develop their own ideal plan for elderly housing in the area. These plans follow a similar typological idea which consists like my own project of a chain-like plan configuration; each one, however, with a specific spatial arrangement. I feel that the idea is both promising and fulfilling. When an elderly occupant moves into one of the little houses the shock of moving away from familiar surroundings is here minimised by virtue of the proximity of the residents to each other and to the landscaped exterior. An identification with the new setting is strongly encouraged.

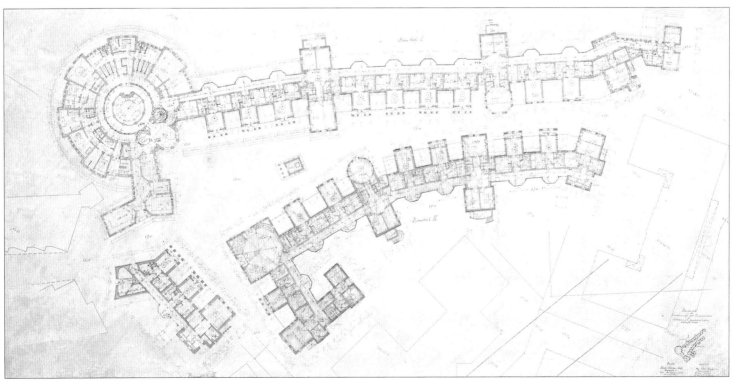

OPPOSITE: VIEW OF THE CHAPEL; *FROM ABOVE:* CHAPEL FACADES; PROJECT ELEVATION; PROJECT PLAN

OPPOSITE: SKETCH OF THE CHAPEL INTERIOR; *FROM ABOVE:* STREET VIEW TOWARDS THE CHAPEL WITH THE COFFEE HOUSE IN THE FOREGROUND; VIEW OF THE PROJECT ENTRANCE

dernière conception de
la nouvelle place de la mairie à Reims — avec Tonci et Léon 10.1.90 à hier

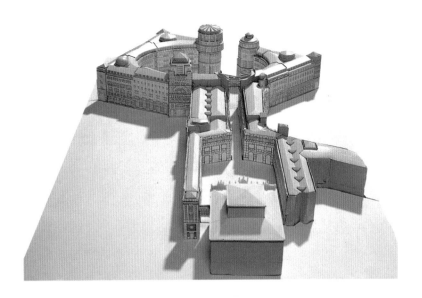

URBAN INTERVENTION IN IRUN

SPAIN, 1988-91

The Basques set fire to Irun before it was taken by the Falangists during the Spanish Civil War. As punishment, Franco made sure it was not rebuilt – unlike Guernica, which he had allowed the Germans to destroy. Now, however, the time has come to heal the wound. This scheme places two squares onto the elongated site. One square has an official character, and contains the town hall; the other has arcades and shops on the ground floor, and housing above. The long arcaded Rathausplatz is ended on the far side by the town hall which terminates a longer axis that leads into the oval Market

Square. This rigid geometry is broken by the positioning at the entrance to Rathausplatz of figural spaces. At the entrance to the oval square two towers stand guard acting as a gateway to the project. It is possible to move through the site entirely under the protection of the arcades, which are treated variously as a system of superimposed orders or simpler rusticated piers. The complex geometry at the edges of the site is counterbalanced by the regular form of the squares and the straight-forward axial sequence, which acts an organiser for the entire neighbourhood.

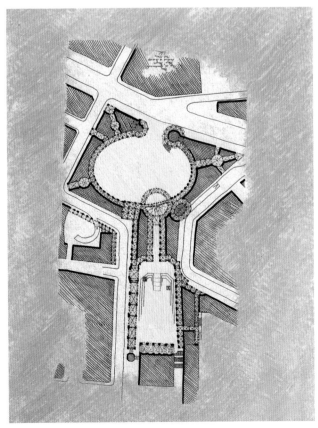
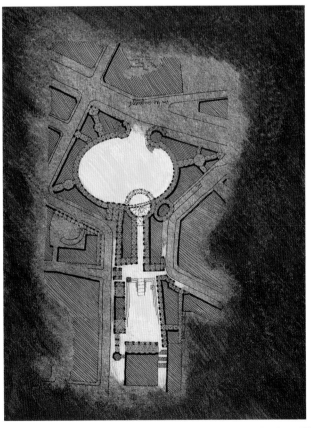

OPPOSITE: VIEW OF THE CURRENT SCHEME FOR THE RATHAUSPLATZ; *FROM ABOVE L TO R:* MODEL OF THE PROPOSAL; PROJECT PLAN IN 1989; PROJECT PLAN AFTER DISCUSSION WITH LEON KRIER, 1990

120

KIRGATE MARKETS
LEEDS, 1989

A well known building complex from the 1930s at the heart of the city of Leeds had to be demolished 20 years ago, due to structural considerations. The hill on which it was situated was exactly on axis with a large boulevard and here we proposed a terminus which would also act as a crown for the city. The axial focus connects down from Quarry Hill to the proposed Market building which is designed as a replacement for the old Kirgate Markets which fell victim to fire 17 years ago. Of the older structure only a limited historically valuable part could be saved and re-incorporated into the new building. A substantially more beautiful complex can now be realised which connects the Market to this old adjacent warehouse. The new structure is designed to nestle up against the historic building and complete the disrupted fabric of the city. On the side of New York street a long facade is interrupted by entrance recesses which lead into skylit corridors surrounding the main roofed area. The urban pattern runs throughout the building, allowing patrons to cross from one side of the site to the other in comfort. The mall hall backs up against the wall of the existing building which acts as a reminder of the old Kirgate Markets in their heyday. The plan is symmetrically disposed on either side of an axis that leads out past an amphitheatrical space and across St Peter's street to the new building at the top of Quarry Hill. In doing so, the Market is indirectly connected back to Eastgate Boulevard to the north of the site.

OPPOSITE: SITE MODEL; *FROM ABOVE L TO R:* SITE PLAN WITH THE NEW KIRGATE MARKETS; VIEW IN THE NEW MARKET BUILDING; VIEW DOWN MAIN GALLERY SHOWING THE CONNECTION TO THE MARKET BUILDING

den Haag   Laus square composition   Krier 91

122

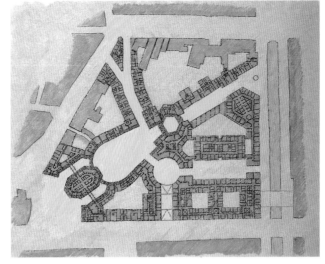

URBAN PLAN FOR 'LAVI-KAVEL'
THE HAGUE, NETHERLANDS, 1988-93

The area of Rotterdam between Richard Meier's new town hall, Rem Koolhaas' dance theatre, and the central station manifests all the typical characteristics of unresolved post-war urban planning. Giant objects stand around unrelated to each other, and each new addition seems purposely to obscure the last vestiges of the relationship between the cultural centre and the station. Only the Lavi-Kavel in the centre offers a real chance for a significant repair of the urban fabric. The basic essence of my urban plan has survived to date, despite the large number of interested parties. But the incredibly strong economic pressures in this area throw into doubt my dream of realising a small-scale residential development. At ground level and internally the roof of the hall is all in timber with a *series of massive trusses left entirely visible. The large teardrop shaped square is ended by a tall tower, breaking the sense of enclosure that is created by the continuous street facades. An axis is set up diagonally against the primary geometry of the site and the surrounding urban fabric. A perpendicular cross-axis intersects the site and separates the main square from a smaller polygonal enclosure. It is thus possible to move practically in all directions across the site. The urban blocks that are created between these streets conceal inner courts, which act as focal points for the surrounding buildings. The new station hall is vaulted and skylit and can be seen as a roofed square of sorts organising the surrounding spaces. The new public spaces provide an indispensable sense of place.*

OPPOSITE: CURRENT MODEL OF THE MAIN SQUARE; *FROM ABOVE L TO R:* STREETS AND SQUARES; PROJECT PLAN; THE HOUSES; VIEW OF THE FIRST DESIGN FOR THE MAIN SQUARE; SKETCH SHOWING CURRENT DESIGN FOR THE MAIN SQUARE

MASTERPLAN FOR PORT MARIANNE – CONSULS DE MER
MONTPELLIER, 1990-93

Ricardo Bofill recommended that I develop further a masterplan he had drawn up for the new town of Port Marianne, next to his Antigone quarter. The essential features of Bofill's plan were in full accordance with my philosophy of urban planning. I had only to make a few adjustments to the massing of the blocks and introduce some details to enrich the plan. Here at last I had the opportunity to develop the work I had begun in Berlin 15 years before. The streetscapes are richly varied. Different architects have designed different buildings – a maximum of four each, scattered through-out the quarter and never clustered together. Similar rules were applied to the developers. I was involved in forming the squares and designing prominent buildings.

'Consuls de Mer' is the first part of the new development to be built. It is oriented towards the old town and contains around 2,800 flats, offices, shops and the usual public facilities. The new town as a whole will contain four different quarters, each with its own distinctive central square, thereby providing a sense of place for each community, as was the case in pre-war towns throughout the region.

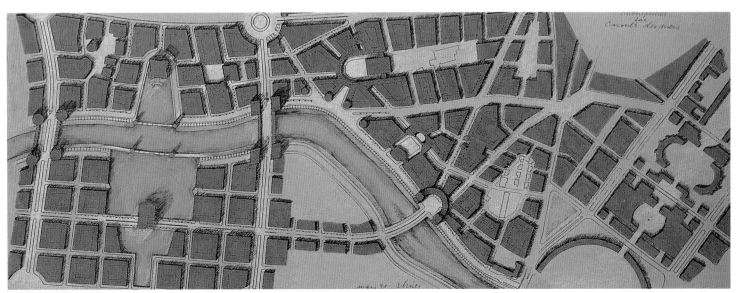

OPPOSITE: MODEL VIEW; *FROM ABOVE:* VIEW OF THE IRREGULAR SQUARE WITH THE CHURCH ON THE LEFT; SKETCH OF THE SQUARE; SITE PLAN WITH BOFILL'S ANTIGONE AND THE NEW TOWN OF MARIANNE

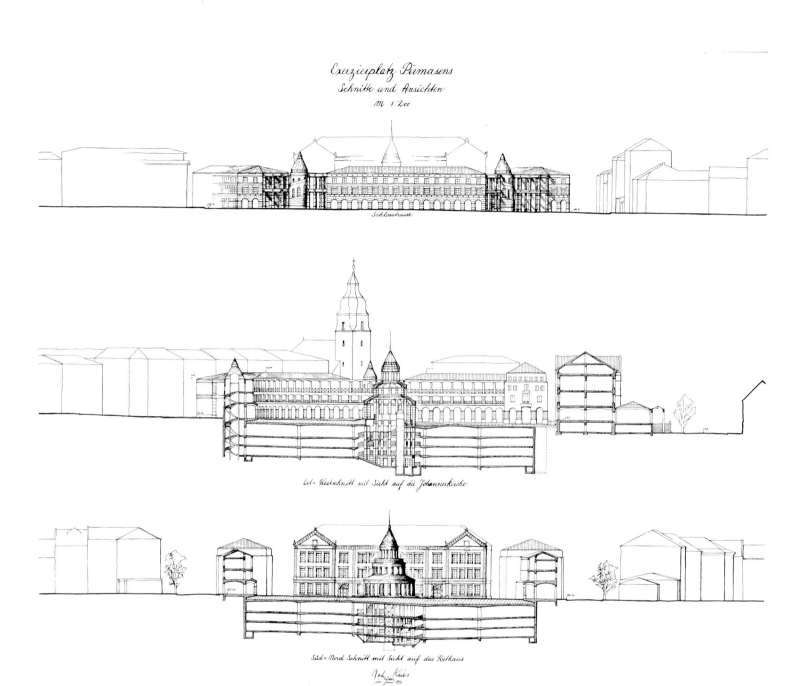

Exerzierplatz Pirmasens
Schnitte und Ansichten
M 1:200

Schlosstrasse

Ost-Westschnitt mit Sicht auf die Johanneskirche

Süd-Nord Schnitt mit Sicht auf das Rathaus

126

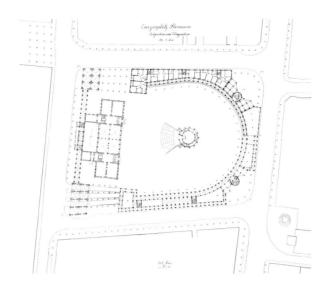

PROPOSAL FOR THE EXERZIER PLATZ
PIRMASENS, 1990

The construction of an underground parking garage in front of the town hall offered the opportunity to change decisively a square that had never recovered from extensive war-time *damage. The sad facades of the postwar buildings were pleasing to no-one – my proposal for the Exerzier Platz indicated how the square could be given a new face.*

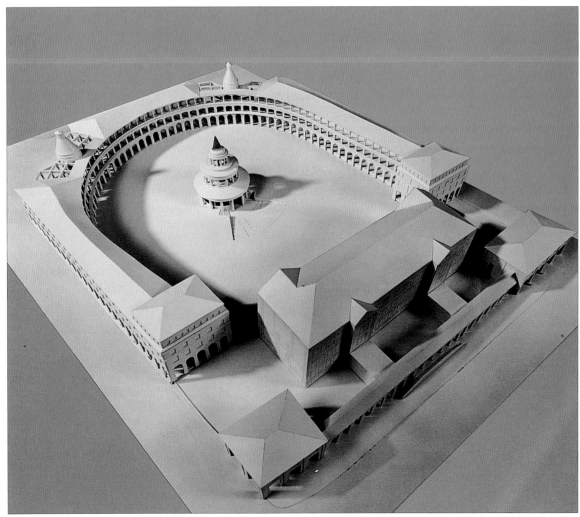

OPPOSITE, FROM ABOVE: PROJECT ELEVATIONS; PROJECT MODEL; *FROM ABOVE:* PROJECT PLAN; MODEL VIEW

MASTERPLAN FOR VENTA BERRI
SAN SEBASTIAN, 1989-90

The new district of Venta Berri is ordered by a clearly hierarchical system of the streets, squares, buildings and vistas which are comprehensible to the 'man in the street' without further explanation. This urban pattern of streets will complement the existing and future streets to the north-west in such a way that new and old streets form a visually cohesive mutually responsive and cohesive whole. The internal street pattern of Venta Berri is determined firstly by the intention of giving the new quarter a strong feeling of centrality and

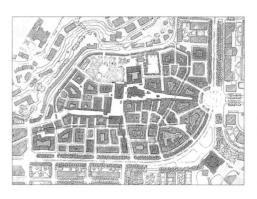

secondly by the new streets adopting the line of geometry of paths, streams, walls and other important local traces which will give the new development an undeniable local character and morphologically founded identity. Four central pedestrian streets radiate from the plaza centrale forming the backbone of Venta Berri into four individual quarters which each have a tree-planted square at the centre. The music conservatory theatre and tower form the visual focus of the plaza centrale. Venta Berri thus becomes its central symbol and landmark.

FROM ABOVE L TO R: VIEW OF THE MODEL; SITE PLAN; VIEW DOWN STREET TOWARDS TOWER; THE MAIN SQUARE

URBAN PLAN FOR GÖTEBORG
SWEDEN, 1989-90

The new neighbourhood is developed around both sides of a former shipyard. To allow as many houses as possible to have views of the water, we created a ring-like canal pattern with an island at its head. The island contains all the cultural facilities and forms, along with the market-place opposite, the focal point of a neighbourhood strongly dominated by wa-ter. The blocks are rather irregular in shape and nestle as close as possible to the polished cliffs of this coastal landscape. Public squares provide smaller local foci for the project and the individual blocks contain green courts. The system of canals and inlets permeates the plan, making islands of certain neighbourhoods which also contain tree-lined streets.

FROM ABOVE L TO R: SITE PLAN; MODEL VIEW; PLAN SKETCH; VIEW OF THE MAIN SQUARE WITH THE MARKET HALL; PLAN SKETCH

130

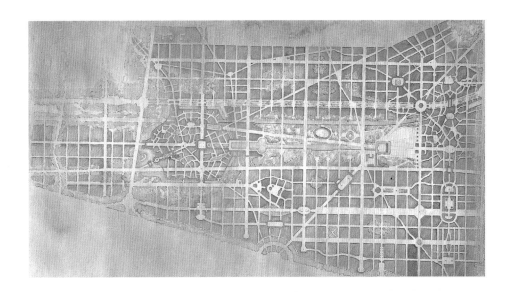

BUSSY ST GEORGES
MARNE-LA-VALLÉE, PARIS, 1989

We were asked to base our study on a street grid of large blocks, 400 metres by 350 metres; established by the official planning body of EPA-Marne after long years of careful development. My only objection was that the plan eliminated both a network of existing paths across fields and a diagonal street that cut through the whole of the new district. Our solution was to overlay the new grid onto the existing street pattern, conserving the historical pathways on this high plateau of the Ile de France and at the same time creating a rich and varied spatial structure. For environmental reasons, we were required to provide a certain area of water as a secondary reservoir. We did this by using a moat to enclose and define the centre of the town. The moat is connected

diagonally, through a large central park, to an old, Louis XIV moated castle. The town centre has housing for 10,000 people and is divided into five different neighbourhoods, each with the requisite public facilities. In this project we used a variety of forms for the blocks, as we wanted to show that a modern town can be an attractive place to live, and not just a concentration of housing for the working population. The spatial variety of the centre is maintained in the outlying areas, which are placed in a ring around it. Each suburb is focused around a central green space. However, this plan departed too radically from the official EPA-Marne approach. In essence, it made the basic tenets of modern urban planning seem foolish. And that was going too far . . . the plan had to remain a dream.

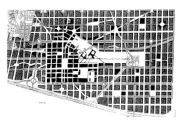
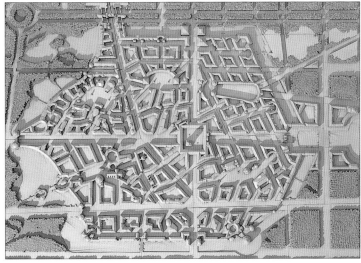

OPPOSITE: MODEL OF THE CITY CENTRE SEEN FROM THE EAST; *ABOVE:* GENERAL SITE PLAN OF THE CITY OF BUSSY ST GEORGES; *BELOW CENTRE:* MODEL OF THE CITY CENTRE;
SURROUNDING IMAGES, FROM ABOVE L TO R: COMPARATIVE CITY CENTRE PLANS INSERTED INTO BUSSY ST GEORGES: LUXEMBOURG, FLORENCE, TURIN, MUNICH

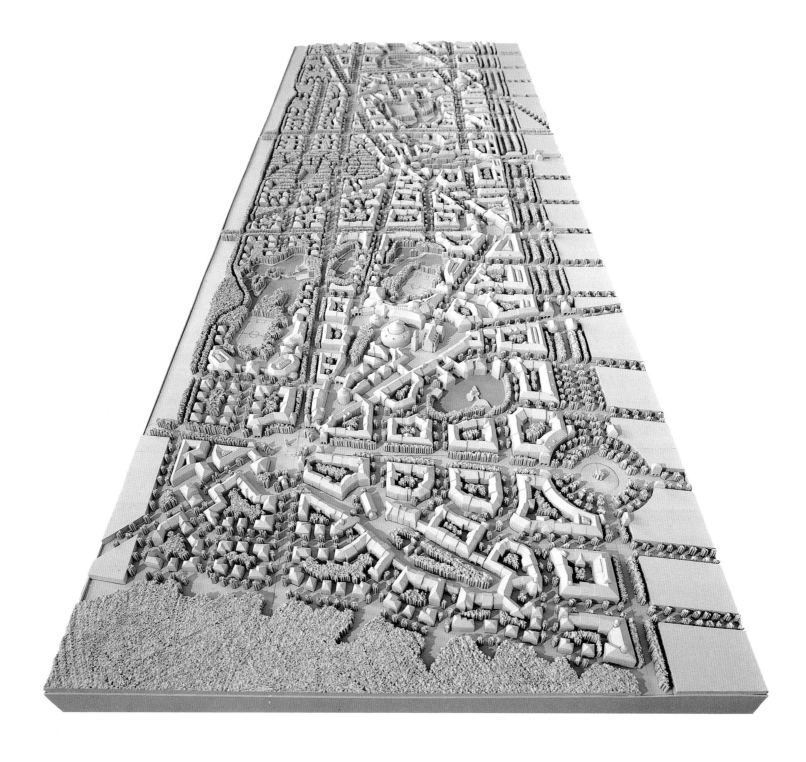

OPPOSITE: MODEL VIEW; *FROM ABOVE L TO R:* THE MARKET SQUARE WITH THE TOWN HALL TOWER; RAILWAY STATION SQUARE;
HORSE-SHOE SHAPED SQUARE; IRREGULAR SQUARE

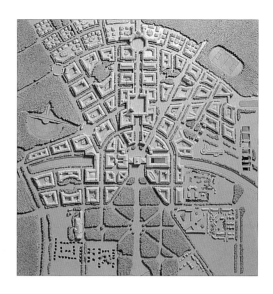

URBAN PROPOSAL FOR CERGY-PONTOISE

PARIS, 1989

We were given a challenging commission to prepare a development plan for the area of the town around the railway station – a similar task to the one at Bussy St Georges, but without such a unified character. Our plan, however, sank without a trace, and certainly without a discussion – an experience my brother had also had in this place years ago.

The scheme consists of a large axis emanating from the railway station and interrupted by two enclosed squares at the intersection with two perpendicular avenues. The station acts as the centre of a radial system of roads which lead to the periphery of the development. Here a large amphitheatre and sports stadium have been situated in the open landscape. The urban blocks are all provided with inner courts. The residential and commercial units occupy the periphery. On either side of the main boulevard large greens have been designed to serve as focal points for each neighbourhood. These are roughly oval-shaped, landscaped gardens bordered by tree-lined boulevards off which feed smaller streets. The radial and axial systems endow the plan with richness and emphasise the peculiarities of the site. On the other side of the railway station a large park picks up the axial system.

FROM ABOVE: VIEW OF THE MODEL; BIRD'S EYE VIEW OF THE MODEL

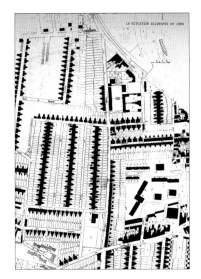

MASTERPLAN FOR BRUAY
FRANCE, 1990

The Mayor put the question: 'How can our "model" town – a turn-of-the-century mining community – be turned into a normal, well-functioning neighbourhood?' The town consisted of rows of tiny brick houses, often so densely packed that they formed a terrace accessible only via a long passage.

Our solution was to form the rows of housing into blocks, creating a regular urban structure with streets and squares. This allowed most of the existing houses to be preserved, with demolition necessary only where the block required a corner building.

The blocks were scaled so as to allow that present-day necessity – the garage – to be placed in the centre, along with gardens and a small public playground. As the model clearly indicates, each new block has a solid street frontage which helps to define the public spaces and streets. Landscaping will also play an important role with gardens and parks located throughout the plan.

This plan could serve as a model for countless similar industrial towns, demonstrating how a 'housing scheme' can become a true 'community'.

FROM ABOVE L TO R: EXISTING PLAN WITH ROW HOUSES; TRANSFORMED PLAN WITH ITS TRADITIONAL BLOCKS, STREETS AND SQUARES; VIEW OF THE MODEL, NEW BUILDINGS INDICATED IN RED

NEW PARLIAMENT BUILDING
LUXEMBOURG, 1990-91

The new building is to be located in the heart of the old town of Luxembourg, on the site of the old Printz metalworks, next to the present Chamber of Deputies and the Grand Duke's palace. It is intended to replace the 19th-century chambers which can no longer keep pace with the requirements of modern government. The existing parliament will be refur-

bished to form an extension of the palace, taking on new representative functions. The square in front of the palace will assume much greater urban importance when the new parliament is built. The significance of the building's function will be underlined by a tower-like elevated structure. The dialectic established between this tower and the belfry in the palace complex is obvious – the opposition of the two symbols is intended to commemorate the successful practice of constitutional monarchy in Luxembourg. On the side of the Rue du St

Espirit is the main amphitheatrical auditorium, which connects on its circular side to the elongated 'Salle des pas perdus'. This four-storey tall space is skylit and intended as an organiser for the entire building. On either end are two large staircases which lead to the upper floors, which in elevation are differentiated by a system of superimposed orders. The tower elevation consists of a large 'Palladian' arch accessed by a monumental stair. Smaller openings perforate the upper floors, which are distinguished by a vertical ordering system resting on a rusticated plinth. The two curved arms on either side of the tower tie the buildings into the surrounding urban fabric and isolate the tower, making it a monument in its own right. By straddling the Rue de l'Eau and intersecting the perpendicular Rue du Marché aux Herbes it becomes a landmark for the entire area.

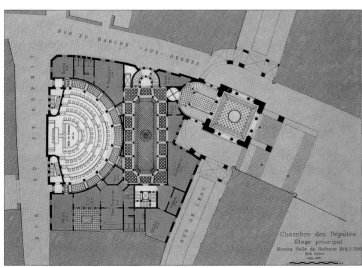

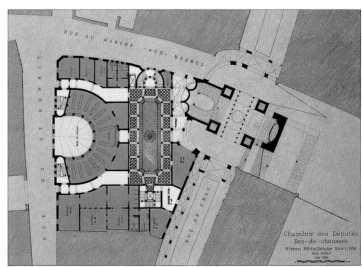

OPPOSITE: PERSPECTIVE VIEW OF THE NEW TOWER; *FROM ABOVE L TO R:* THE NEW PARLIAMENT HALL; SECTION THROUGH THE BUILDING; PLAN AT THE LIBRARY AND ARCHIVE LEVEL; PRINCIPAL LEVEL WITH THE PARLIAMENT HALL

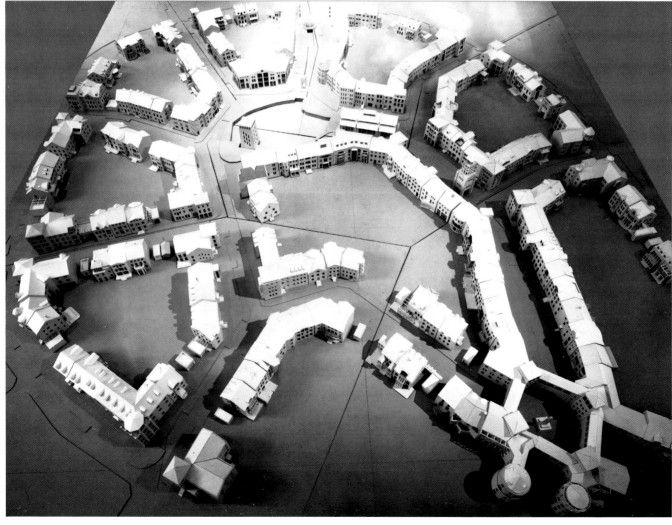

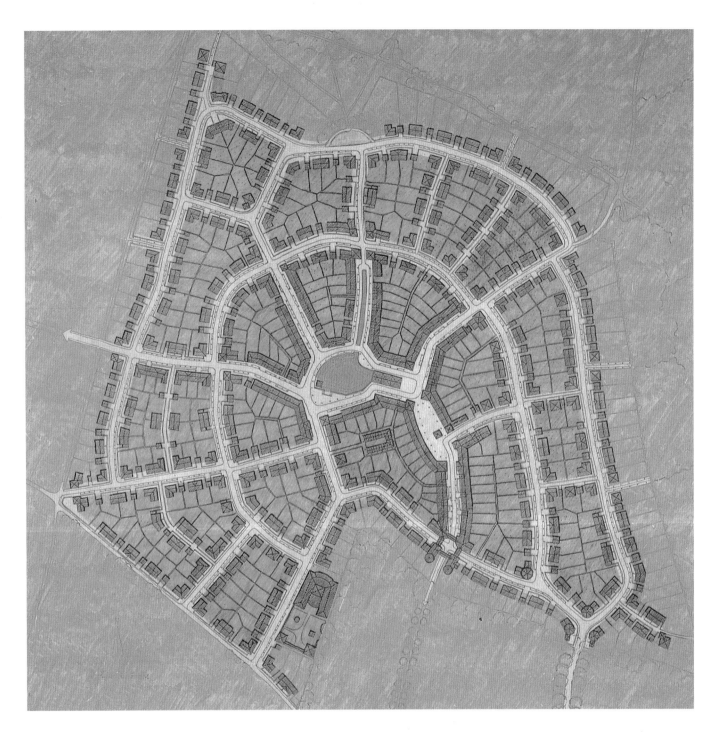

NEW COMMUNITY IN POTSDAM-EICHE
BERLIN, 1991

This is a proposal for a new community of 500 families close to the gardens of Potsdam castle, on the northern edge of the Eiche district. The houses are grouped very loosely around a defined centre. The gently concave landscape of the site and the existing picturesque street pattern gave rise to a correspondingly soft typological grouping, which avoids strong axes. I also felt it was necessary to

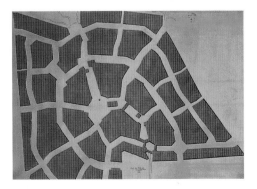

avoid making the all too obvious association with the geometric order of the neighbouring classical park. At the end of the main radial road at the south-eastern end to the development, a square becomes the sole urban element in the scheme. As this marks the main approach to the site it acts as an organiser from which the different parts of the estate can be reached and assumes the role of a gateway.

140

NEW TOWN AT POTSDAM-DREWITZ

BERLIN, 1991-93

In planning this new town for 7,000 to 10,000 inhabitants, our main concern was to establish the strongest possible link with the community of Drewitz to the west and the 'lowland' development to the north.

We worked around two important existing features: the 'Hirtengraben' *in the centre of the 56 hectare site, and the wonderful* 'Priesterallee', *with its old oak trees. The motorway is lined with a large 'clean' trading estate, which serves as both a barrier against traffic noise and a source of employment for the families in the town.*

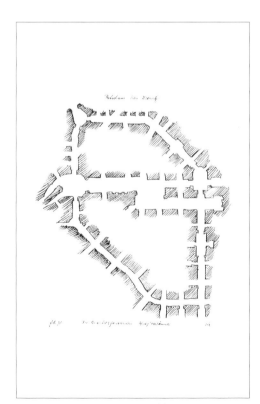

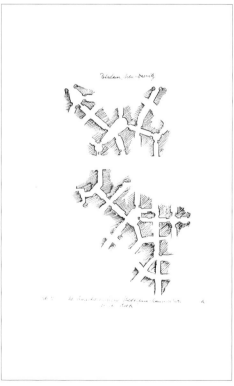

OPPOSITE, FROM ABOVE L TO R: BIRD'S EYE VIEW OF THE CITY GATE SEEN FROM THE NORTH-WEST; CITY GATE SQUARE; VIEW ACROSS THE POND; *FROM ABOVE L TO R:* SITE PLAN;
PERIPHERAL BOULEVARDS WITH THE CROSS-STREETS; SQUARES; INTERNAL QUARTER ARRANGEMENTS

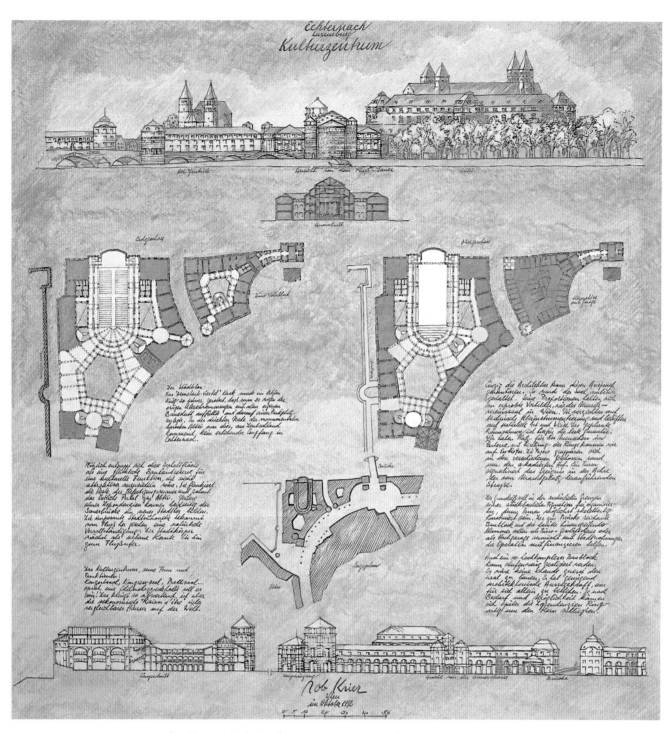

CULTURAL CENTRE IN ECHTERNACH
LUXEMBOURG, 1992

I was particularly pleased and surprised to be asked to design a cultural centre right next to the Baroque abbey in Echternach, for I spent six years of high school in the town, and it still holds many memories for me. Here, in front of my old classroom window, I have my very own building site!

The community has undertaken an ambitious project, with plans for a large assembly and banqueting hall flanked by meeting rooms for a variety of organisations, a small museum and shops, etc. We chose to base the building on the model of the abbey, adapted to meet the required new functions. Along

with this complex, a new town gate is to be built on the old Roman bridge. The site is roughly triangular and intersected by a road flanked by two towers. The main auditorium is an elongated horse-shoe shape which connects onto a hexagonal court open to the elements. This court acts as a cloister, much like in a monastery, and together with the auditorium or great hall organises the entire building. The shifting geometries of the site are negotiated by round nodes or halls. At the entrance of the building a tower rises above the roofs and helps to balance the imposing shape of the great hall.

OPPOSITE: CONCERT HALL, CULTURAL CENTRE, ECHTERNACH; ELEVATIONS, PLANS AND SETTING OF THE CULTURAL CENTRE

POSTSCRIPT

This book can unfortunately only hint at what I would like to have achieved in practice, during my 30-year struggle for a valid conception of urban development structures and integrated clear housing typologies. For many years, vehement criticism of my work and defamatory public disputes consumed an excessive amount of my energy and time. When I did get the chance to build, the modest budgets (for the social housing for example), along with the undermining of the architect's authority in the construction process, effectively ensured that my ideal concepts were realised only in schematic form.

I still find it miraculous that I had the chance to build two real squares: the Schinkelplatz in Berlin and the Camillo-Sitte Platz in Vienna. 20 years ago, when I was working on the *Urban Space* book, I would never have believed that I would be so lucky. Though these places are modest in scope, I know that they will provide a fitting setting for public life, blossoming with time and growing old grace-

fully. No architecture critic's commentary could give me an equal sense of success. My very traditional approach to architecture and urbanism sets me – and a few friends – far apart from successful mainstream architecture at the end of this millennium. Still, we have had time to prepare our theories well, to separate our ideas from ever-changing fashions, and to lay a foundation for building in the future.

My teaching activities have taken up much of my time, but they have also given me the means to try out different theories and strategies. My work as an architect has had a distinctly 'applied' character. I have never had the opportunity to advance to the higher ranks of the profession and produce public buildings such as town halls, museums, churches and schools ... the true realm of the architect. I have gambled a lot and lost a lot. This book bears witness to that. Yet ideas can have strength even if they remain unbuilt. I hope that my drawings, along with their practical message, will recall something of the visionary dream.